Etiquette
for girls

DEBRETT'S

Debrett's Etiquette for Girls
Published by Debrett's Limited
18–20 Hill Rise, Richmond,
Surrey TW10 6UA
United Kingdom

Debrett's Etiquette for Girls, an idea
created by Jo Aitchison and Eleanor
Mathieson

Managing Editors
Jo Aitchison
Eleanor Mathieson
Liz Wyse

Design concept and style by Officelab, NYC
Page design by Design 23, London
Additional design by Yahya El-Droubie

Proof reading and index by Ruth Massey

Publisher Ian Castello-Cortes
Chairman Conrad Free

ISBN 1 870520 87 4 / 978 1 870520 87 4

Printed and bound in Portugal by Avarto,
Printer Portuguesa

Visit us at www.debretts.co.uk

Etiquette
for girls

Dear Stephanie,

Happy Sweet Sixteen

All our love

Tina, Gary, Ben,

Harry, Caitlin & Jonathan

xxx   xxx

FLEUR BRITTEN

DEBRETT'S

Contents

Introduction   6

Social Graces   8
The Basics   10   Fundamentals of Friendship   18
Deportment   12   Friend Management   20
Silent Signals   14   The Art of Giving   22
Public Manners   16

Image Management   24
Basic Principles   26   Shoes   38
Conduct and Style   28   Accessories   40
Wardrobe Rules   30   Perfume   42
Make-up   32   Formal Dress Codes   44
Hair   34   Occasion Wear   46
Underwear   36

Food and Drink   48
Table Manners   50   Lobster   62
Table Settings   52   Principles of Wine   64
Canapés   54   Wine Behaviour   66
Messy Foods   56   Champagne   68
Sushi   58   Spirits   70
Seafood   60

Day to Night   72
On the Move   74   Formal Dinners   86
At the Gym   76   Bar Behaviour   88
Salons and Spas   78   Club Culture   90
Paying Your Way   80   Sociable Smoking   92
Restaurant Behaviour   82   Elegant Drinking   93
Paying the Bill   84

Special Occasions   94
Festival Chic   96   Perfect Picnics   106
On the Beach   98   Polo   108
On a Yacht   100   On Stage   110
On a Private Jet   102   Meeting Royalty   112
Hotel Behaviour   104   Meeting Celebrity   113

Man Management 114

First Moves 116
Flirting 118
First Dates 120
One-Night Stands 122
Blind Dates 124
Staying the Night 126
Playing the Plus-One 128
His Friends 130
The Mini-Break 132

Meeting the Parents 134
On Holiday 136
Couple Conduct 138
Infidelity and In Flagrante 140
Saying Goodbye 142
The Ex and No-Shows 144
Understanding Men 146
Proposals 148
Rules of Engagement 150

At Home 152

Perfect Hostess 154
Drinks Party 156
Dinner Party 158
House Guests 160

Good Guest, Bad Guest 162
Flatmates 164
Country Guests 166

Face to Face 168

Introductions 170
Graceful Greetings 172
Clever Words 174
Conversational Quicksand 176

Tools of Conversation 178
Troublesome Talk 180
Gossip, Bitching, Lies and Excuses 182

The Written Word 184

Invitations 186
Essential Stationery 188

Written Communications 190
Email 192

Getting Ahead 194

Office Politics 196
Office Survival 198
Office Romance and Sleaze 200

Handling the Boss 202
Good Boss, Bad Boss 204
Socials and Away Days 206

Fundamentals 208

Golden Rules 210
Picture Credits 212

Acknowledgements 213
Index 214

Introduction

For many of us, life is just too fast to bother with manners. Bombarded with news and communication, our reflex is to scuttle through and get it over with. Civilities, inevitably, are the first thing to go. Discretion is out because notoriety seems like so much more fun. The vestige of social responsibility that remains is confused as we are flooded with wildly contradictory global customs, leaving us to slump in apathy when it comes to doing the right thing. Yet in a world of ever-increasing social mobility, knowledge of etiquette is more necessary than ever.

While the definition is rather more loose than it used to be, and the practice rather less obsessive, social conventions still guide us towards what is acceptable behaviour. Snobbery lives on, but fortunately, managing social scruples is no longer a hidden code. Searching for guidance is an accepted and ever relevant pursuit.

Etiquette is a revisionist business. Social change is now infinitely harder to keep up with (no thanks, in part, to the recent communications revolution). There are ever more ways to commit a *faux pas*. New rules are constantly appearing and old ones evolving. What was frowned upon just ten years ago is the done thing nowadays. Society may be more liberal about certain things, but perfection now has new parameters. Getting it right is not just about following form, but about understanding the spirit in which the rules were written.

Thus, a modern survival manual is called for, to lay out the new social order and explain how to ensure damage limitation. Social success lies in forethought and understanding. Back by popular demand, etiquette has re-entered the zeitgeist. Be sure that you are switched on and prepare to prosper.

Social Graces

The Basics

Beyond being true to oneself, many of one's social obligations are met simply by making others feel at ease. Be sure to consider others' feelings, be kind, remember people's names and extend a personal touch. Respect should be mutual, compassion should reach right to the margins. A ready smile is an easy and excellent first defence in almost all awkward situations.

Manners make life more bearable. They are there to conceal our selfish, childish instincts. Manners are mutually advantageous to giver and receiver, so create a virtuous cycle; rudeness does the opposite. Manners are an agent for positive engagement and for getting more out of people. They are enabling and disarming. Here, there is plenty of moral merit and personal gain to be had, and better still, all for free.

Of course, good manners should come from the soul, but a contented veneer will ease relations around you, so a dose of disingenuousness is easily defensible. This behaviour can be very quickly learned. Smile, say please and thank you and laugh appropriately. As a result, people (whether they take it as the truth or see it for what it is) are most likely to be nice back, genuinely or otherwise. A good-humoured glow will envelop all, everyone is happier and often the performance segues in to the real. N.B. restraint is key here. Melodrama and mawkishness will only kill the effect.

In certain situations, obedience is far less useful than outrageousness – take thrilling conversations and wild parties for starters. Slip-ups can make for occasional light relief. Sometimes politeness is a hindrance. Forbearance and stoicism might move us up the stairway to heaven but are no good for assertiveness. The application of good manners is largely situation-specific and there is much room for personality and free will. Take note of the people who surround you, however, and be sure to carefully heed their expectations.

Tradition still advocates (rightly) that certain people should be treated more equally than others. Older generations, professional superiors and high-ranking individuals deserve extra respect. There is also a positive correlation between age and increasingly exacting rules. It is usually too late to teach old dogs the new, more relaxed way, so it's only polite to meet them on their side of the generation gap. Do not begrudge them this; remember that ready smile.

Deportment

Good posture makes you look taller, slimmer, perter and more confident. It gives you better presence. Think tall. Hold your head high, keep your back straight, shoulders back, tummy in and hips forward (remember that invisible piece of string pulling up from the top of your head).

Do sit properly. Jiggling, tapping your foot or swinging your legs (as with all fidgeting) tends to infuriate. Shoes off or feet up on furniture is regarded as most improper. For perfect and old-fashioned ladylikeness, sit with knees together, ankles crossed, and lean very slightly to the side. For the most basic ladylikeness, at least keep your knees together. Indulging vanity publicly by staring at your reflection or partaking in excessive posing, pouting and preening will always appear rather desperate.

Space invaders who breach others' personal space can induce anxiety and prevent relaxed social intercourse. Be sure to keep your distance: the normal minimum gap between you and others should be a comfortable 45 cm. Rules are bound by situation, however: in crowds and noisy places, there is no choice but to be cosy. The opposite is true in offices. Here, violate someone's space and you threaten their power as well. If fiercely protective of your own space, keep others at arm's length by holding an object such as a glass out between you and the perpetrator.

Queues possess their own unique rules. Don't stand too close to those in front of you (especially at cash points). Confronting queue-bargers will get you to your rightful place, but the moral high ground tends to be a much safer,

more satisfying and less embarrassing place to stand. Doors should always be held open for people, though it's more rude to do this if they are at a distance (they then feel obliged to break into a trot to reduce your waiting time). Limit it to those who are directly behind you. Always thank anyone who holds the door open for you. In lifts, avoid staring at people (direct your eyes towards the middle distance), don't engage in any cringe-making conversations (note that the cringe threshold is very much lower in a lift), don't use mobiles and don't treat the person standing closest to the lift controls like a bellboy. Say 'would you mind getting five?', not just 'five, please'. Hold the lift for those who are running to catch it and let people out before getting in. Withhold all personal habits for the duration of your ride.

Simpering daintily is (thankfully) no longer called for, but being ladylike is ever valid. There are, of course, poise, language and charm to consider, but more of a concern is exploiting your rights in the two parallel realities that women occupy. In the rarefied world of old-fashioned manners, there is still preferential treatment to enjoy; in real life, you should expect a fight for equal opportunities. Overdoing fake girlishness – laughing in all the right places, toying with one's hair, avoiding controversy – won't advance anything but your love life. Sitting, walking and standing like a woman, however, will make you appear (and feel) in control and confident. Enjoy the elegance of femininity and benefit from the added respect and attention that grown-up posture will bring you.

Silent Signals

We are complete emotional giveaways. Before we even open our mouths, little speech bubbles are leaking out from all over ourselves. These stem from our posture, gesticulations and facial expressions. Unless we are primed in this unspoken language, we can easily reveal things that we would rather not. With a little bit of knowledge, however, those speech bubbles can be easily and cleverly overwritten.

Closed body language can seem like a social barrier. If you are looking to engage with the people around you, avoid double-crossed legs and tightly folded arms, eyes fixated on the floor and hunched shoulders. Open body language – palms upturned, extended eye contact – is more conducive to sociability. Leaning away while resting your head on your hand can show a

level of disinterest; leaning in with your head tilted indicates the reverse. Nodding encourages conversation, as does smiling, and proves attentiveness. Overzealous nodding (or smiling) will tend to obstruct it. Mirroring the body language of a companion indicates a real connection, but is easily faked.

Facial expressions are the biggest betrayer of emotions. Hide them under a social smile; contrive genuineness by flashing a glimpse of teeth. Don't frown – it is terribly ageing. Maintaining eye contact implies confidence as well as control; staring is quite unsettling, particularly if at others' inadequacies – birth marks, cold sores or comb-overs. Likewise, 'elevator eyes' (i.e. the up-and-down) are extremely disconcerting. Gazing over someone's shoulder when in conversation is just plain rude. If told

to look at someone nearby during a conversation, wait a minute and then swing a panoramic view, taking note at said position. Pointing at people or whispering behind hands makes others feel insecure.

Even in these unchivalrous days, you will occasionally encounter a man who insists on holding doors open, standing when you enter the room and helping you with your coat. Some modern girls may take offence at these gestures: increasingly alien, they can feel like an affront to our feminist convictions.

Rejecting the 'ladies first' gesture may be commendable in principle, but it can also be considered churlish (and is baffling for men). Don't be afraid to enjoy these feminine perks. Charm will get you through most eventualities, including this maze of gender politics.

Public Manners

Poise

Elegant composure and dignity are two essential protective shields behind which you can play the world with an air of confidence and control. This is easier said than done, however, as perfect poise takes insight. Moods must be managed; exasperation, irritation and boredom repressed; sermonising and superiority banished.

Public altercations and emotional downpours are instant poise-crushers. Save all high emotion for home. Good turn out – dress, hygiene, grooming – and a collected manner are highly persuasive. Squawking and screeching are less so; excessive female birdsong must be muffled. Keep a handle on the volume, especially in enclosed public spaces. Don't imagine that others will take any interest in your chat. Turning up talk for their benefit is indelicate.

Society and the Self

By all means let it all go behind closed doors, but in public, your reputation is at stake. You are your own brand – reining in your less endearing vices not only protects others, it's vital for your own social progress.

The most advantageous position in a society where manners are frequently overlooked is to expect the worst yet hope for the best. Don't waste time on small-minded concerns or petty point-scoring. When friends desert us at the final hour, say, serving them a taste of their own medicine only encourages them to do the same again.

Instead, remain philosophical. The best weapons here are forgiveness and equanimity. Manners take morality and generous spirit. This is not martyrdom, but giving the benefit of the doubt and realistically, it's the only option.

Punctuality

While punctuality may be rather more relaxed nowadays, being 'fashionably' late will only ever be rude (the fashion industry is not exactly celebrated for its compassion). Dare to keep an obsessive timekeeper waiting and prepare for a curdled encounter.

The need for punctuality depends on the situation. For one-on-ones in public, it is unfair to leave a companion looking unpopular for an hour – aim to arrive inside 15 minutes. If meeting at someone's home, things can be more casual, but not so casual that dinner is ruined by the time you appear.

For 8-for-8.30s, it is imperative to make it by 8.30. Arriving early is never going to look cool but is advisable for formal appointments, job interviews, travel, performances and ceremonies. Never turn up early for a dinner party.

Modern Variations

Mobile phones may enable the luxury of progress reports if running late, but don't take advantage. Letting friends know that you won't be there on time doesn't justify the act. In the same way, the gift of social or physical brilliance does not, as some are led to believe, excuse lateness.

Progress reports must be accurate. Ten minutes means ten minutes, and not thirty. Of course, mobile phones can be thanked for facilitating brilliantly spontaneous gatherings. It is fine to be a little lax if all members are aware of the form, but don't be tempted to use mobiles on more formal occasions. Don't be a pushover with inveterate latecomers, instead, think about implementing some training. Let them know that you feel put out or just start without them – that will teach them.

Accountability

Without this, even the mild-mannered can appear selfish. Not showing up when expected will always be taken as an insult. Honour all of your promises, answer your phone, respond to emails, turn up on time. Disrespecting an arrangement looks arrogant and throws consequent plans out of sync. Late cancellations must be made by phone. Email or text is not acceptable here. Only when you hear your companion's voice can you be sure that they will not in fact be sitting alone, waiting for you patiently.

Last-minute cancellations must be suitably compensated for. In the case of double bookings, always honour the first commitment. Double shifts – where you dash from one engagement to the next – should be downplayed (or you are likely to face socialite accusations).

Fundamentals of Friendship

It is probably our dear old friends who get us at our rudest. Social niceties are superfluous around such familiarity, or so goes the thinking. Friendships are surprisingly fragile, however, and good friends deserve to be kept sweet more than anyone. For something so bound in free will, there are a certain number of obligations. At the root is that most sanctimonious of concepts, give and take. Taking is the easy part; giving may require a little effort.

Rubbish friends break promises and good friends are good to their word – smart people don't make promises in the first place if they are uncertain. As unappealing as they may be, birthdays, weddings and other important events are obligatory. Bailing out when not in the mood or double-booking with better offers are not options. Prepare

to make some sacrifices, especially in their time of need. Real friends are obliged to deal with the bad times, or face the tag of fair-weather friend.

Favours (that may sound more like impositions) will be asked of you. Try to console yourself a little with the honour of being asked; bank your credit for a rainy day. If you are asking the favour, don't ask something of someone that you wouldn't do yourself. Don't make generous friends wait for your thanks. Reward them there and then (a dinner or present are suitable). Incentives are far more enticing than guilt trips.

Looking out for friends should be an ongoing concern. When out for the evening, rescue friends from bores and nanny them if they don't know anyone. In correspondence, any wall of silence should not be taken as an affront. It

might be that the friend is just busy but they could also be unhappy. If they are suffering real problems, intervention will sometimes be required. This is a most delicate situation and it might be wise to seek the counsel of others before barging in. Show a bit of thought and make friends feel appreciated. Send newspaper articles of interest, news of a play they might like or remind others of upcoming birthdays.

Life envy is often inevitable between friends. A friend that perfectly matches you (in looks, salary, wit) is impossible to find, but you should be pretty equally balanced. If the balance tips, then any resentment must be deeply buried. If you feel that you are left playing catch-up, think of it as a good game-raising asset to be seen around such success. Avoid the temptation to turn into the

friend. Picking up on their habits, dress style or mannerisms is never an option.

If your find that you get on better with someone your friend introduced you to than you do with the original friend, what is the form? Surely no one would notice if a quiet little friend affair was conducted? If your bypassed friend is male, there is usually no problem. Try to steal a friend from a girl and expect to be summarily excommunicated. Girls are much more territorial. The good-friend thing to do here is to include the original friend in all situations.

If your friend is flirting threateningly with your boyfriend, either avoid seeing her when he's around, or tell it to her straight. He may also be encouraging matters so keep calm and don't just lay into her unquestioningly. When friends turn into frenemies, or when common ground crumbles away, there are two ways to give them the heave-ho. A silent termination is usually preferable to the dull ache of chronic sufferance. Simply drift away; don't return their calls or emails. Prepare excuses if you bump into them. Their feelings should still be protected, especially with this karmically questionable behaviour.

When an impasse is reached and there is little to lose, having it out can offer resolution and clear the air. This is probably best conducted in public in order to avoid any unladylike shouting, hair-pulling or swearing. There may be a chance that the misguided one will see sense, and that all can be friends again, but it is often fatal. The ensuing fall-out can become awkward amongst mutual friends, so if in doubt, always opt for the freeze.

Platonic friends can sometimes get the wrong idea. Boys will misread the signals and they will try their luck. If a male friend is knocking on the wrong door, either hint at your disinterest or break it to him gently. Hinting is often preferable – to be any more explicit can seem arrogant. In addition, hints are less indelible and are more likely to fade away. A direct conversation will leave a much deeper impression. With more thick-skinned types, sometimes frankness is the only way. Both of these approaches need to be gently guided by sensitivity.

The easy route is to freeze him out. Distance yourself physically; delay your responses; never sign off with kisses. Avoid getting very drunk and staying up late together. As a last resort, affect ugly habits in front of him.

Friend Management

Uncomfortable Truths

So your best friend has food stuck in her teeth. Do you tell her? Of course. Any situation where friends will benefit from the truth is reason enough to be honest. But the truth does hurt, so your delivery must be judicious and always tempered with positives. Sometimes a gentle tease – rather than being too gloomy about things – is the kindest way to approach the situation.

In more serious circumstances (e.g. their long-pined-for ex has got a new girlfriend) be careful not to tempt them into shooting the messenger. The truth-telling must be tailored to your friend's sensitivity, and done in private. If your opinion is invited, then provide. They ought to be prepared for it, but this will also elicit defensiveness.

In situations where the truth might help prevent friends from making very unfortunate mistakes – such as clothes shopping – feelings must be forsaken. When it is too late to do anything and feelings are likely to be hurt, however, white lies should be mobilised ('no, you look absolutely lovely!').

Brace yourself. If you are handing out truths to all and sundry, you may get some back. If you put friends on the spot, be prepared not to like what you hear. At least be mature enough to accept criticisms without argument. It might be instinctive but it will never be excusable. If you already suspect the truth (yes, you have put on weight), then don't subject friends to this test.

Apologising and Forgiving

Pride is the nemesis of humble pie, but without that little word 'sorry' many friendships have disintegrated over the tiniest trifles. It's often more productive to be kind than to be right. Delivery must be sincere and never overstated, a little meekness helps. For particularly evil sins, consider accessorising your apology with a gift or gesture. Gifts shouldn't be abused as Get Out Of Jail Free cards, however, as only a change to the offending behaviour will afford lasting atonement.

If you feel that your moral compass can't yield to accepting blame, then a small olive branch will be better than nothing. Also note: a rapprochement can never come too late.

Grudge-bearers would be wise to be comforted by the selfish gains of forgiveness. This act starts to unravel the knot of negative baggage at once. It may take more effort, but it is much more gratifying to look down from the high ground. Bitterness only eats away at the soul. Don't wait around for the apology that will never come. If the sin is friendship-cleaving (think hateful lies, infidelity, stealing) then a showdown is called for. Allow them to explain; to stew only harms you.

Accepting friends for what they are and tolerating their foibles is a sensible long-term model that should ultimately make for a smoother ride (if tougher in the short term). After all, perfection can seem so two-dimensional.

Compliments and Playing Fair

Compliments are like social credits. Don't just think them to yourself, pass them on and buoy others. While girls may get away with their ritualistic rebuff of compliments from other girls, boys tend not to grasp such self-deprecation. Here, a simple 'thanks' will do. Whether complimented by boys or girls, don't blurt out how much something cost or which very expensive designer made it; information on bargains is rather more welcome, however. Compliments that ring hollow or seem backhanded should just be accepted graciously.

Sportsmanship is important among friends, as excessive competitiveness is most unladylike. If playing for pleasure, tone it down or face being relegated by your friends to the proverbial subs' bench. Victory for Type A personalities is hollow – it only serves as a warning to others that playing with them is not fun. Being the team player is much more likeable. Winners should play down their glory. Victory dances only suggest the novelty of your winning; good losers always congratulate the winner, and both get over themselves quickly.

Refuse to be riled by others' one-upmanship. Encourage them not to take things so seriously but think twice before disputing the score. Cheating is for those incapable of winning on their own merits. It might pay, but minus a sense of honest accomplishment it's an empty honour (cheating can be used only to sabotage other cheats).

The Art of Giving

Giving is not entirely selfless as there's always a lovely warm glow for the donor to enjoy. While present-giving should be discretionary, unfortunately there are some situations that demand it.

If you can't attend the grand event, you are still obliged to give a wedding present. Even if you have sent off your telegram and even if you won't get your part of the bargain with that gourmet banquet, duty remains. It is acceptable to boycott wedding lists (and especially wedding 'funds'), though any off-list gift must be extremely imaginative.

Birthday presents really should be non-optional. That said, they're largely neglected and are therefore an easy way of being the very thoughtful friend. Births must be honoured, while house-warmings and Christmas are mainly for those closest to you.

You can't just give any old thing, as limp gifts are embarrassing. The perfect present requires very special consideration and attention to various elements. While it's not what you have but what you choose to give, measured generosity is always appreciated. Don't bankrupt yourself just for the sake of keeping up. Instead, club together with others or make something (provided it doesn't resemble a shabby playschool offering). Boring can be preferable to brave. Play it safe with tokens, candles, books, plants, edibles or drinkables if you are not very well-acquainted with the recipient. Try to steer clear of the over-obvious; flowers can look a little thought-free after the 37th bouquet of daffs appears on the labour ward. Chic wrapping and a handmade card will raise the calibre of a humdrum present.

Re-gifting is generally disapproved of, but can work if you are careful. No one must know. If the original giver will notice the gift in question's absence or could find themselves in the company of the new recipient (and gift), then re-gifting is rather reckless. Other dangers are if you've evidently used it, or if you can't remember who gave it to you. Re-gifting should only be resorted to if it's the perfect thing for the recipient, and not just because it coincided with your spring clean. Multi-gifting – giving the same present to numerous recipients – is a touch lazy but fine if said recipients never meet.

Try to admire the brutal honesty of someone who is openly unimpressed with your gift. Giving them the receipt will save you the bother of re-launching the tiresome hunt for the right thing.

If you're receiving a present from somebody, your delight should be unambiguous and all-accepting. Even if you hate it or have it already, tact is best. You can always consign it to the re-gifting cupboard. If you're very close to the giver and are sure they are thick-skinned enough to handle the blow, then confess your disappointment. If some candour is appropriate, or if your dislike could be noticed ('darling, you never wear your lovely sunshine yellow twinset'), then tell the donor. Saying that the item doesn't suit/fit you, rather than it being entirely unlikeable, is the best way of maintaining goodwill.

N.B. you'll generally need to throw a party to maximise your present count. Asking for money may get you money, but it could also get you a few sneers. Don't forget your thank you letters.

Image Management

Basic Principles

The unfortunate truth is that society judges first on surface. Doubtless, such superficies will jar with our more high-minded ideals, but clothes have instant social implications. Making friends with fashion is a Hobson's choice, yet what a two-faced friend. It champions both creativity and freedom but, at its core is a conservatism that speaks of must-haves and must-nots. Its rule book is closely guarded by a secret society of beautiful freaks, leaving the rest of us to fumble blindly and await ridicule. At its most cruel, fashion is a tyranny that makes women feel inadequate. It is a moving target: the harder you try, the easier it is to miss.

We may aim to rise above fashion and side with its more mature sister, style, but they are congenitally joined. Style can't exist in isolation. If we must

dance with the devil, it's very important to be able to second-guess the pitfalls and capitalise on the perks. Ensuring there are no chinks in your armour is essential for good damage limitation.

Prominent among the plus-points of fashion is its ability to empower you. High glamour can open up the velvet rope, power dressing can open up the career ladder and dressing pretty-sexy opens men's eyes. Forms of effective non-surgical intervention – towering heels, illusory cosmetics, genius pattern cutting, clever underwear – are at the disposal of those who need a quick helping hand.

Dressing is a method of instant messaging. Forget asking for a cup of sugar or a light, there isn't a healthier icebreaker than an interesting outfit. Clothes say all of 'look at me', 'look

don't touch' and 'come hither'. Those playing the dating game might like to employ touchy-feely fabrics (cashmere or silk) as a tactic to make men melt. The psychological perks are numerous. Retail therapy is much cheaper than a psychiatrist and clothes can be mood altering. Dress playfully or sternly and the appropriate mood will follow. Any experimentation is fun, while fabulous clothes are a confidence pill.

These virtues, however, don't erase fashion's pitfalls. If you wish to emerge unscathed don't believe the hype. A healthy disrespect for fashion is most imperative. Fashion is a religion and branding is all about belief. The hype would make label slaves out of all of us, but the reality is that the emperor's new clothes will be re-invented every season. We must learn to see through

them and ignore the nagging voice of unreason that talks us into making foolish fashion choices. Remember that glossies give fake advice; pictures are falsified with bulldog clips, flattering lighting and airbrushing. Learn to pick and choose, as working a head-to-toe look is the very worst in fashion clichés.

Prepare to be judged and damned if you do make an effort (as narcissistic, profligate and obsessed with style over substance) and damned if you don't (as square). Watch out for *schadenfreude*. We are all greatly amused by others getting it wrong and then resent those who do get it right. Remember that fashion time is much faster than real time and sell-by dates are even shorter. One final thought: fashion and flattery are not mutually inclusive, as fashion really has no mercy.

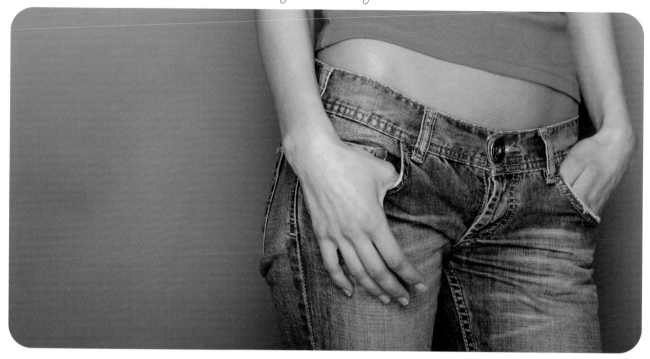

Conduct and Style

The trials of fashion become far more complex when it comes to borrowing clothes. Cherry-picking garments from friends' wardrobes definitely requires a certain skill.

An accomplished borrower rotates around a well-sized lending pool and keeps lenders sweet by volunteering suggestions in reciprocation. She will always return garments within a week, lovingly washed in accordance with the care instructions. If a button falls off or any other mishap occurs, she will fix it and may even over-compensate with a token gift. For her efforts she will be rewarded with limitless resources. But a bad borrower, on the other hand, never confesses to any damage caused, or worse, never returns the garment. This is tantamount to theft, though it's not considered at all rude for lenders to ask for their items to be returned. Bad borrowers will be silently punished with black marks and firmly held grudges.

Borrowing clothes at least keeps things upfront. Some girls believe that it is a waste of time to trawl the streets when stylish friends can showcase the best buys, leaving them to follow suit with maximum efficiency. Replicating the odd piece is limp but acceptable (and can be flattering to the friend), but head-to-toe cloning is plain creepy. If there is any chance that the two of you could turn up to an event looking like carbon copies, take action to eliminate the risk. Whoever bought it first gets first refusal.

Competition is tough out there, so while anonymity can be useful (e.g. on Sunday supermarket sweeps), a girl sometimes needs to stand out when she enters a room. For these occasions, fashion has a plentiful arsenal of secret weapons to plunder. Consider vintage one-offs, red lipstick, hats, or any other form of well-pitched outrageousness to be your turbo button. If you get it right, a hum will bubble up across the crowd when you first arrive, strangers will then approach you and much attention will ensue. A calm self-assurance will be required to pull off the high-visibility strategy, but it will be repaid in higher denominations of confidence.

How does one decide between the moneyed look and stealth wealth? It's easy to confuse gaudiness for luxury, even if couture clothes can show status. High-maintenance dogs' dinners are never a good look and conspicuous consumption is very dated. You should at least work towards 'effortless' effort.

Wardrobe Rules

There are two choices. You can either wear what you damn well like and feel comfortable, or strive for that tenuous equilibrium of trying to get it just right, without trying too hard or not trying at all. The latter is a much more complex business requiring a balance between appealing to both boys' eyes and girls' eyes, between comfort and effect and between exposing all and none of your assets. Ensure that you never do legs, cleavage, big hair, make-up and heels all at once; this is so very obvious.

When stocking the wardrobe, lazy classics are your allies. Jeans and white T-shirt is the uniform of icons on dress-down days, and fail-safe standbys for when you can't be bothered. 'To diet for' pieces are the enemy. Don't be in denial about your dress size: bulging out of too-small clothes does not grant automatic inclusion into that size. Any clothes that are obviously ill-fitting are equally ugly. Hems and cuts should sit as intended.

Waiting list pieces are pure fodder for conformists. By the time your name is up, there will be lookalikes (not to mention fakes) all over. Do all you can to dodge the *doppelgänger* effect by spurning the allure of any must-haves. Instead, aim just under the radar and achieve maximum singularity. Learn to indulge in foreign shopping sprees, love small chic independent labels or, for sure-fire tailored originality, invest in your own seamstress (by which time you really have arrived).

Respect your own colouring or defy it with good make-up. You must strike a balance between hard and soft (neither the dominatrix look nor chocolate-box sweetness) and avoid literal time travel with vintage. In fashion, one can never say never, except to thigh-high boots, yellow tights, pleather, 'babe' slogan T-shirts, bustles and jeans aged in pools of household bleach.

The tricks of the fashion trade are yours for the taking. Vertical stripes and block colours slim and elongate, while floaty skirts flatter big hips. Open shirts, V-necks and long necklaces all point to the cleavage. Black will remain the only miracle panacea that slims and absorbs lumps whilst remaining eternally chic. Anyone who finds that a single extra millimetre of width is a calamity should choose finer denims and needle cords over workers' jeans, jumbo cords and tweeds. Acquaint yourself with the ill-advised. Avoid bagginess on both top and bottom, three-quarter length skirts and trousers on shorties and stripes that are unflatteringly horizontal.

When dressing, aim for showroom condition. Neat pressing is optional but there should be no dirt, smells, frays, bobbles or rips (unless artful). Watch out for marks from deodorant, fake tan and make-up; attend to any spillages instantly. Consider your audience and never intimidate or disappoint. Carry out essential checks before facing your audience. Do you look like you got dressed in the dark? Do the colours go together in daylight? Does your coat clash or complement? Are you good enough to photograph?

Any clothes that demand constant tugging, straightening and hoiking will diminish your intellectual presence, so road test them at home. Dance in the mirror if needs be. Pin and tape where required. Heed *le derrière* danger zone: you can't see what we can see and we can usually see straight through white linen trousers and skirts.

Wearing tight white jeans, thin silk or chiffon skirts or unlined satin on top of cellulite always invites trouble. Even in the dark, sheer fabrics worn without sufficient petticoatery look cheap, not insouciant. The same applies for muffin tops (i.e. tummy spills) and shirt-strain. Anything his 'n' hers is very disturbing, as is lamb dressed as mutton (almost as much as the other way round). Any flesh on show should be well-groomed; keep second-rate body-parts tucked away well out of sight.

Be brave and break the rules. We all want to fit into our respective tribes but, above all, try to be original. Learn to delight in a good clash. Embrace the perfection of imperfection; relish the accidental outfit and haphazard style. Indulge in a bargain but never become a high street clone. Invest some time and effort; off-the-peg window-dressing is mask-like and impersonal and it only reveals compliance. So, throw off your doubts and take some risks, but don't let that look wear you.

Make-up

Assisted beauty is a blessing, yet what ugly truths lurk beneath this façade of loveliness. Beyond pure conceit, it is even possible to argue the selflessness of cosmetics. In the workplace, hiding blemishes and bags creates a pulled-together and professional look and, in the street, it persuades others that we live amongst the pleasures of beauty. The fact that it also makes us more confident can oil the wheels of society. Bad make-up is worse than no make-up, and bad usually means too much (think cabin crew or cosmetic counter chicks). Many women are slaves to the slap and, like weight, it can easily pile on unnoticed over the years.

That 'fresh-faced' is the opposite of fully made-up suggests enough about its potentially ageing effect. Reduce your dependency and try to appreciate a little bit of what nature intended. Too much is tacky; aim for variety. You don't wear the same outfit every day, so why wear the same make-up? Within the limitations of what suits you, a change makes for a pretty surprise and will also prevent that make-up pile-up through acclimatisation.

Daytime *maquillage* should only be as much as is actually needed. Work at the no-make-up make-up look. For the evening, use your secret weapons to garner mass admiration, but never go out all guns blazing. Scarlet lips here, false lashes there, but don't ensemble unless taking to the stage. Ready for a close-up? In one-on-ones, keep a few windows open (clean lips or dewy skin); a full face mask can distract and even frighten. Day-to-evening events require midway maintenance. Only apply high voltage tools (colour eyeshadow, liquid eyeliner, lipstick) at sunset. Commit to occasional maintenance during the day to stem the inevitable slide southwards.

A bit like the magic circle, killing the illusion by publicly revealing the tricks of make-up is not on. Why do women open their mouths to put on mascara? Who cares, but it's never pretty. Active vanity should be hidden from view and also from the early throes of romance.

Try out foundation in cruel daylight before you buy. The right shade (on the arm, hand, chin) is invisible. Face tone must match hands and neck, unless you are possessed of an unfortunate ski tan. No tidelines and no mismatches should be a no brainer. If you are cursed with unfortunate spots, check concealer by a window for believability before leaving the house; prettied eyes and tumbling

tresses are effective diversionary tactics but don't overcompensate with too much slap. If make-up goes blotchy or is smudged, start over as patch-up jobs look just that. If it's all looking heavy, a spritz to the face will help melt make-up into dewiness. Contouring make-up will fool no one at fewer than 50 paces.

Eyelashes are the window frame to the soul. For a fitting tribute, cover with a couple of coats of mascara using a not-too-loaded wand. Pay some extra attention to outer corners and avoid creating great solid lines, clogging and hairy spiders' legs. Eyeshadow is the cheetah of make-up – good for sprints but bad on marathons. Any creased eyelid is as ungorgeous as greasy hair but sadly inevitable in sultry climes; use a neutral eyeshadow base to delay the slide. If your eyes have it, ease off on

your lips. Brows must always be a plural. 'Natural' is nice, furry caterpillars not. A decent eyebrow wax is an instant facelift (a beauty magazine cliché and quite true). Over-plucking is terribly unsightly; never attack eyebrows from above. Trim long unruly hairs – pluck at own risk of bald patches – and aim for symmetry.

Lipstick is the high heel of make-up, so heed these proverbial grates: avoid lipstick on any drink receptacle, strong lipstick in the office, lipstick on cracked lips and rampantly kissed red lipsticked lips. Novices should define boundaries with a lip pencil, fill in with a lip brush and blot (a little powder on top reduces feathering). Always carry a mirror for teeth/smudge checks.

Nails should never be dirty, acrylic or more than 3mm long. They should

be shapely and of equal length. Never wear nail art, nail jewellery or French manicures on toes. Sandals mustn't be worn without checking pedicure status first. Impeccable nails tend to read as high-maintenance: perfect for snaring a boy who understands diamonds.

If only there was an appreciation of pale and interesting; fake tanning is so very problematic. It not only reeks, but it collects in the hairline and eyebrows, on corners (knees, elbows, ankles) and in webbed bits (toes, fingers). If you risk a home job, exfoliate and moisturise thoroughly first, and remove any excess after application. Always, always wash hands. The biggest danger is fake tan blindness, where obsessives don't know when to stop. With so many hazards, those of kabuki white complexions are best advised to pay the pros.

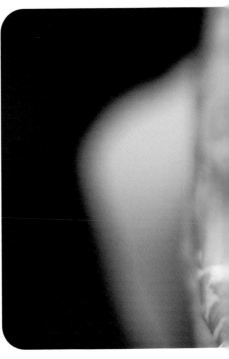

Hair

Once upon a time, hair was there only to keep the head warm. Nowadays its purpose is largely aesthetic and what you choose to do to it forms a unique signature. Unlike a steady hand, hair is harder to control; it is mostly helplessly beyond one's peripheral vision.

Hairdresser monogamy increases the chances of a good hair relationship. You should be safe in the well-tipped hands of a trusted regular stylist. Salon promiscuity may mean never having to tip, but unfamiliarity makes us say yes (I really like my new haircut) when really we mean no (I asked for a trim, not a strim). Be vigilant with rebellious stylists for the sake of customer rights, and try to avoid fashion salons that only craft locks into one of the textbook styles of the season. Clothes will be cold-read by the stylist, so if you don't want to

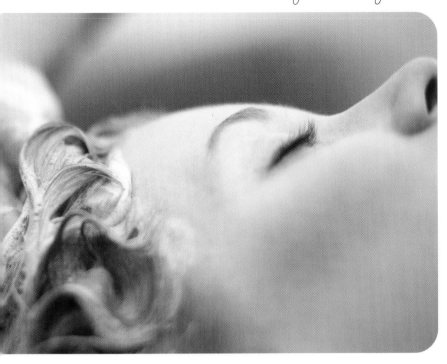

come out looking like a trendoid, leave the fashion numbers (or, conversely, the tracksuit bottoms) at home.

The best hair has nonchalance, i.e. a hot cut that needs little maintenance. Know your hair (e.g. fringe on wavy hair demands daily preening) and your face (no pixie cuts on chubby cheeks). Get more bang for your buck by asking for a blow-drying lesson or demonstration of other ways to style your hair. Feeling sociopathic? Your nose in a book says 'do not ask me about holidays' and a magazine says 'possibly interruptible'.

When tipping, both the stylists and colourists should be tipped five to ten per cent of the cost of the cut/colour, handed over in cash when paying the bill. The hair washers should receive a couple of pounds into their hands after washing your hair. Salon owners usually

allow grace on tipping as you have already had to stump up for their own vastly inflated rates.

The following are brown paper bag scenarios that should be avoided in the name of self-preservation. Greasy hair is a friend of laziness (and rockers) but what can look passable in the morning usually slides into shameful disarray by evening. Greasy fringes are the female equivalent of the five o'clock shadow. Avoid becoming the victim of a bad dye job. Chronic blonde ambition can result in blonde blindness, leaving hair looking ashen. Thick blond stripes on brunettes won't deliver more fun. Don't skimp on maintenance; roots on show are never permitted.

Hair no-nos include: bunches and Heidi plaits on women of a certain age, very ornate up-dos (unless at your own

wedding), tacky extensions and creepy fake hair bands. Helmet hair is the very antithesis of style (ration that hairspray); very tight, high ponytails are uncouth. Boyish cuts, coupled with tomboys' clothes and no make-up, can be very misleading. Long, hip-length hair looks narcissistic and obsessive and usually ends up tangled.

Flowing locks aren't suited to open-top cars or speedboats. While a high-speed drive-by may impress spectators, the end effect (knotted, polluted and matted) won't. Employ a tasteful outfit coordinating headscarf.

Don't shake or swing your locks like a shampoo model. Constant fiddling and hair-twirling will only reduce a girl's perceived IQ, while animalistic head-scratching is most indelicate. In both cases, beware of dandruff.

Underwear

Underwear is underwear is underwear, so underwear as outerwear is a most regrettable fad. Regardless of your own private audience (even if non-existent), high standards will reap rewards. Treat yourself like a thoroughbred and you'll feel like one. Remedial scaffolding can improve posture, but ill-fitting undies can wreck a silhouette. Eyes love a flaw and, in this case, it's bulges and dents. There is no room for any sentimentality about pants; their shelf life is finite. So any that are sagging, frayed or greying should be summarily decommissioned.

Have your bra professionally fitted. We don't want to see bra straps falling down to elbows nor such tight security as to cause welts or VBL (very unsightly indentations below the armpits). You'll need to bare all up-top, so throw aside your modesty while the fitter measures underneath and around the fullest part of your bust. If the back of your bra sits higher than the front, it is too loose. Avoid any slippage by buying fitted to fasten on the widest catch; tighten as it stretches with age. Hand-washing will prolong a bra's lifespan, so is worth the effort, but never hang near heat to dry as this ruins the elastic. Unstructured bras only look cute on nubile petit pois breasts. Learn to love underwiring. The more support, the less they will droop. Take advantage of the engineering of balconette bras on occasion.

Don't over-expose. Sagging boobs in plunging tops are unsightly. Flashing bra straps on formal occasions is most disagreeable. Pretty bras can get away with an airing when worn with the right look, but no one cares to see wide matronly fixtures or clear plastic straps as we're not fooled by their invisibility. Wearing sheer shirts that reveal bras underneath is brazen exhibitionism. Be careful that push-up bras don't make cantilevered bosoms reach chin level and don't always be inclined to upsize. An over-padded bosom can look like a torpedo, while creating a cleavage out of nothing just looks abnormal.

Lacy bras under tight tops read as an unfortunate craggy skin condition so wear smooth cup. Wearing a white bra under white clothing is considered sloppy; go with a nude bra instead. Tit tape rarely lasts the night, especially in sweatbox clubs, so take spare supplies. Gravity can send (cheap) strapless bras waistwards. Giant sticking plasters from department stores tend to have more staying power. Chicken fillets can be most effective for enhancing your bust

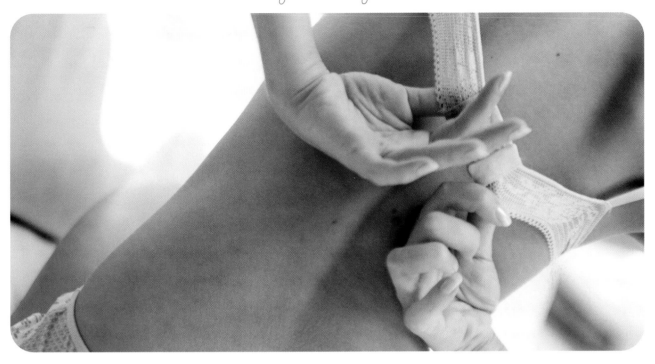

dimensions. Check for comfort and fit before wearing. You should be able to trust your equipment implicitly.

When it comes to the bottom half, have a nice drawers' drawer. Concede to a couple of matching sets but don't be a slave; cut out labels so they don't stick out. While it might seem insipidly sensible to promote comfort over style, ants in the pants is utterly unstylish. It's a complete fallacy that thongs are sexy, unless on the pert cheeks of a 17 year-old. Wedgie producing knickers should be discarded and never plucked in public. Going commando is a bold act reserved for the confident and brazen; it should remain an intimate secret and never be combined with white fabrics.

Keep the 'whale tail' (the visible 'T' of a thong as seen out the back of low-cut jeans) out of sight. If you do insist on sitting on a tightrope, make sure it's of the hipster variety. Use 'magic' pants to hold in, lock down and smooth out lumps (if you're sure you won't need to reveal them). Never squeeze into a size eight when you are a twelve. Unsightly bulges will inevitably ensue.

Tights are a most unglamorous but functional garment. Try the following unglamorous but functional guidelines to get it right: the shorter the skirt, the thicker the denier, the smarter the do, the sheerer the denier (and the longer the skirt). With peep-toe shoes, wear sandal toe tights (with an invisible toe). Schoolmarmish types insist that ladies should only go barelegged with knee-length skirts or longer. This rings true for office wear, but is very floutable on idle summer days. Don't wear laddered tights. Ditch the tights and go bare if a ladder materialises, or carry a spare pair for special occasions. Spend more on thinner deniers (they are less likely to snag). Beware of strange protrusions from body-shaping girdles.

Boys don't find tights sexy and see flesh-coloured tights as a total turn-off. While men appreciate fishnets/stilettos, it's generally considered a bit tarty. Do expect some people to find stockings slutty (and therefore great for affairs). Avoid patterns unless you have long legs. Watch out for unattractive colours (check shades of 'nude' for unnatural orange or brown hues). Don't wear pop socks if there's any chance you will get caught wearing them; they're best worn well-hidden under trousers and never with skirts. They may have briefly flirted with fashion but were quickly dumped for being ugly. Save for practical use.

Shoes

Heel Behaviour

Rational behaviour can't be relied upon here, considering that most women are prepared to remortgage a house for the sake of modern day foot binding. Only a woman understands the real power of a heel. It doesn't just lengthen legs, increase height and tighten calves and thighs; it also has a direct and positive psychological effect, turning you into Super-You. The trade-off is that normal faculties can be impaired.

In other people's homes, surrender spike heels at the welcome mat for the sake of friendship and any precious new wooden floorboards. Ensure your outfit will not be marred by the removal. The offer to bare all and denude feet should only ever be followed by the unveiling of an impeccable pedicure. Shoe-gazing is, however, self-admiration without the help of a mirror, so desist.

Proportion and Sizing

Appearance isn't superficial, it's a set of profoundly complicated equations. So, heels make feet look shorter, flat shoes make them look longer. Rounded-toe shoes can shorten the foot, while flat shoes can make calves seem chunkier. Stilettos worn with micro-mini skirts are vulgar; short skirts should be tempered with flats or knee highs. Mary Janes with tent dresses appear prudish. Something in between is perfection.

Women, as with their dress size, will often prefer to overlook the heftiness of their feet. Squeezing feet into daintier, smaller shoes is a much worse look than the alternative. The ensuing blisters only worsen the aesthetic; plasters are always unsightly, no matter how invisible. Toes should never be permitted to roll over the edge of sandals. Conversely, feet in oversized sale purchases look comical.

Walking and Balance

When we wear heels, our inclination is to walk with our neck and bottom stuck out and legs splayed. This should be overridden at all costs. Instead, push hips forward and pull shoulders back. Putting one foot in front of the other ensures that catwalk slink; hips naturally flow in a figure of eight. Avoid dragging the feet; land ball first then heel. This also gives better hold in metal heels upon treacherous terrains such as shag pile, gravel, grass, cobbles and marble. Heel pros score the bottom of slippery soles with a knife to create grip, or are never without the arm of a chaperone.

Give your shoes, feet, legs and back a break on long traipses; opt for pumps or slimline trainers. Save sports shoes for the gym or when running, and never ever wear with skirts, unless you're on the tennis court.

Maintenance

It's awfully motherly, but shoes must be polished and clean; re-heel while the tip is still visible. Shoe nuts enjoy that shoe-tree/photograph/box/tissue swathing business which is a little obsessive, but probably sensible. At least try to stuff the toes of more precious pairs.

Sort out smells with odour eating insoles, deodorant or Botox injections (in extreme cases). Those with problem perspiration should accept shorter wear-by dates for shoes and remember that trainers enjoy bath-time in the washing machine. The malodorous should never wear trainers without socks again.

Heel fatigue is disruptive, so while comfort usually comes after style, fun must always come before style. If heels are murder on the dance floor, it's better to dance in flats than have to sit it out in sore stilettos.

Accessories

What is there not to like about pretty decoration? Accessories have form *and* function. They are a very handy device for diverting attention away from bad bits and onto assets, be it swan necks, cleavages or, if it needs be, inoffensive earlobes. They are also a refreshingly democratic one-size-fits-all foray into fashion, offering safe experimentation with more 'ambitious' trends.

Accessories generally fall into two bags: fashion and classic investments. Where your own ratio lies depends on personal taste and the occasion. The classics should ideally be acquired as presents from infatuated admirers and wealthy relatives, though a woman who buys her own diamonds demonstrates exemplary independence. A perfectly-chosen investment is like a great friend: it can be taken anywhere. Watches and decent jewellery are particularly worth dropping hints for.

The biggest danger is overdoing it. Never should a look include more than half of the following: necklace, earrings, hat, scarf, bag, sunglasses, headscarf, bracelet(s), tiara. Resist wearing more than two matching accessories; avoid excess around the head. If you start to feel fashion-foolish, it's easy enough to remove any number without shame. All accessories should be treated to a bath of sorts from time to time.

When it comes to jewellery, cheap stones can be good. Cubic zirconia is very effective as a poor girl's diamond. Buying cheap metals is less advisable as these can smell odd and react on the skin. If shopping for four-figure-plus jewellery sets, work it for all it's worth. You need the necklace, the matching earrings, the bracelet and, of course, the brand. Bigger pieces tend to look silly together. When buying a watch, try to think of when you will wear it. While horolophiles say life is unlivable without at least three – day watch, dress watch and sports watch – if you're just buying one, go for adaptability.

As for bags, a girl really can't have too many. Any stockpile should include various day bags, bijou evening bags and dinky rucksacks for festivals/gigs. No impromptu party girl is without a bag-within-a-bag; like a space shuttle, the command module (and life's many mundanities) can be hastily jettisoned in a cloakroom, while the lunar module is taken into the stellar party. Any bag's contents are a) a bit private and b) a bit embarrassing; keep it zipped and don't pry into others'. Carrying an oversized shoulder bag is like going around with a canoe. Beware of china displays when turning around.

In olden days, hats were a matter of propriety as one would never dream of stepping out naked on top. Now they are a matter of originality. Attention is guaranteed, whether you desire it or not. In with the bargain are a number of subtle cosmetic tricks. Head carriage is lifted and posture improved, eyes and cheekbones are framed, bad hair is concealed and unfortunate face shapes rectified. Down-turned brims and short crowns assist horsy faces, feathers and decoration soften faces that are square. Avoid big hats if short or small of face and small hats if tall. Hats sported with overstyled hairdos can look highly naff. Don't try to kiss in a wide brim. Clever hostesses should angle hats to leave a clear run-up to a cheek. Avoid baseball caps at all costs.

Fitted leather gloves are impossibly elegant, excellent for driving control and for waving adieu to those left for dust. Ideally they're tailored like shoes to feet; don't wear on consecutive days and store flat to prevent any stretching. When choosing belts, fit is less crucial, but be careful of just-so arrangements that require adjustment with every turn and twitch.

Silk scarves are the ultimate desert island luxury. A large silk square can become a hair accessory, a top, a belt, a knapsack, a sarong, an SOS flag and, indeed, a thing to wear around your neck. They are also indispensable as a guardian of modesty in foreign lands, to wear on heads or shoulders. As for sunglasses, shops are surely conspiring against us. Exactly how can we gauge suitability when our vision is obscured by security tags and darkness? Take an honest friend and buy what suits, even at the expense of fashion. Put on when the weather dictates and never wear sunglasses indoors, in the pool, after dark, when talking to strangers or at weddings (so trashy).

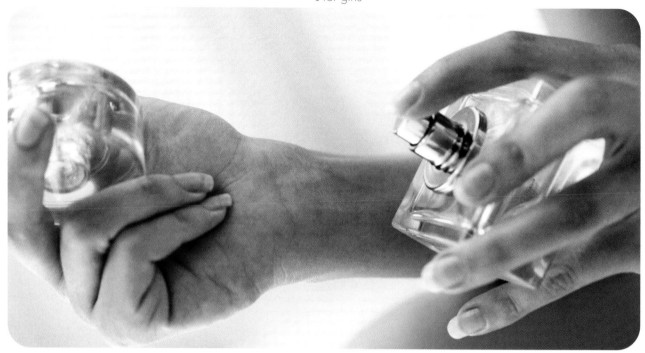

Perfume

Perfumes are the closest science can get to creating personal auras. Money can't buy you a sunshine-yellow halo? There's surely a perfume out there that will say as much and create your point of difference. The perfume you choose is an expression of personality; falling for a brand smacks of suggestibility. As a secret weapon, however, perfume can backfire as it has the power to trigger both love and loathing.

Perfume is a complex mistress. She is easily misunderstood and she easily overwhelms. A problematic parameter when it comes to hitting the right note is quantity, but of course taste is also a factor. The trouble arises when people become immune to their fragrance and allow their perfume to announce them before they arrive, then linger in a toxic aftermath. Tragically, only they cannot

smell the desperation. Ration yourself to a squirt or two; break the spell by not wearing your perfume every day or by rotating a variety. Be neighbourly in confined spaces such as auditoriums, cars and planes, and factor in the time of day. Wear the lightest of lightness in daylight and perhaps something a little richer for when under the moon.

A girl's lair must be subtly scented to maximise male ensnarement. While it may not be good for the self-esteem to know that men's knees turn to jelly on account of a bought-in artifice, girls must learn to exploit such handy tools. When men just can't help acting on impulse, it's down to musky notes working like pheromones. By wearing perfume behind the ears, in the hair, or in gentle diffusion, by spraying it into the air and walking into it, you should

lure them right into the zone. To men, perfume shouts 'notice me'. Used in moderation, it should work like a Venus flytrap, but in excess it's just a turn-off.

Parfum (the most pricey) contains the highest concentration of essential oils, followed by eau de parfum, eau de toilette and then eau de cologne. The higher the concentration of essential oils, the less needed. Remember that perfume denatures faster in heat, light, oxygen and when contaminated by dirt. The shelf life of an open bottle can be just a year. Layering scents sometimes works; easy does it with other scented lotions and potions that your body may require. Cleanliness is an essential base for perfume. Masking unsavoury body odours or the bouquet of unwashed clothes with a heavy scent will create a monster far viler than the original.

Formal Dress Codes

Non-conformists like to balk at such a regimen, but there's reason to obey. As well as reducing dress stress, there's a much broader purpose: clothes impact on behaviour. So, formal attire elevates proceedings, casual dress understates them. Disrespecting a host's preferred aesthetic is an unimaginative rebellion (far more sophisticated to intellectually subvert). Sparkling within prescribed parameters greatly improves chances of unsolicited social overtures.

Dressing to a code is not as simple as painting by numbers, and obstacles abound. Instructions are often woefully under-prescribed (sometimes entirely absent) and are blurred by subjectivity (one girl's Sunday best is another girl's sleepsuit). Nail-biters resort to certain clues: the formality of the invitation, the cause for the occasion and the chosen

location (lavish venue means smart affair). Timing matters; early evening drinks are normally less formal than a dinner/dance. Always dress up rather than down – being the best-in-show is never a major transgression. Employ removable accoutrements for in situ fine-tuning. Impromptu up-dressing is rather more of a challenge. Quick fixes include sculpting a hairdo, scrounging some lipstick and keeping In Case of Emergency earrings in your handbag. The best recovery, however, is the glow of self-confidence.

Black tie is easy for men. For girls, it's likely to entail shopping tantrums and begrudged costs all for the sake of having to expose hang-ups in that most unforgiving of all garments, the dress. Hems can creep all the way up to (just) above the knee but, if so, legs

must be bestockinged. Separates are accepted, though unofficially disdained for letting the side down. If worn, they should be matching and as elegant as a dress. Trousers stand on even shakier ground; the traditional 'do' should be honoured with a bit of skirt, but more modern hosts tolerate superbly styled trousers. Likewise, a deep-plunge dress might not be too fresh for more with-it parties, but any potential indiscretions must be taped into submission.

Resist piling on the paraphernalia as if you've just escaped from a house fire. Go for quality over quantity. Generally, just one striking piece is more voltage enhancing than too many accessories (but this depends on the fickle fashion climate). High heels can add elegance and propriety, but barefoot dancing is inappropriate and bad-mannered in the

44

eyes of the old school (and hazardous). Handbags must be dainty. A warming wrap is essential equipment even if you are planning to fall straight into some hero's welcoming DJ.

White tie is the dress code for the most formal of events, so-called since the male of the species is required to don a white bow tie. Here, nothing less than full-on evening dress will do. Bite iconoclastic tongues and delight in the parade of eccentric traditions.

Unless you have access to the huge dress collection of a princess, such a summons is likely to elicit considerable alarm for the modern girl. As white tie extravaganzas are a rare species, any full-skirted taffeta investments are most ill-advised; it is wiser to borrow or hire. Dresses must be long and hems should just skim the ankle. Cocktail dresses, no

matter how demure/*du jour*, are never appropriate, while arriving in trousers could result in a summary dismissal.

Since legs are enshrouded, it's quite the norm to exhibit a little *décolletage*. Long evening gloves are as standard as wearing shoes (a blessing if prone to excessively perspiring palms). Wearing rings over the top is regarded as rather unsavoury, as is eating in them. Shoes may not often be glimpsed, but they should be as fine (and as comfortable) as can be. Jewellery ought to be the stuff of heirlooms, couture or good fakes. Hair is best worn neat, especially long locks which should not be freely flowing. Handbags should be subtle yet splendidly bijou. As a last bastion of conservatism, coordinating accessories are actively encouraged. Take note and be sure to conform.

Occasion Wear

'Smart day', or 'formal daywear', is the typical prescription for a society event. The terms are hopelessly nebulous as a guide, so one could easily suspect a conspiracy to catch out the nouveau. A little homework to put the event into context (timing, weather checks, venue research) is prudent. The spectrum of formal daywear is seemingly generous, from separates to suits to dresses, and appears to grant plentiful individuality. Herein lies the ample trapdoor for ruinous misinterpretation.

Dresses are the least controversial choice and allow joyous breezes for what is often a summer event. Those preferring comfort and familiarity over effect should be adequately smart for most occasions in a skirt, top and smart cardigan or jacket. But beware, as this freedom is to dupe the dilettante. Stick to two colours and smart fabrics. Linen, by the way, should be outlawed. By the end of a day's scrunching, it is a long way off smart. Soft grass eats heels so stilettos can be problematic for outside events. Skirt or trouser suits add instant formality but are far too dour if they could suit a courtroom. Formality can be offset with delicate embellishments such as corsages, brooches, pretty buttons and various daring accessories.

At more established day events, modernity has little clout. The exact form of dress rules can still be difficult to predict, however, as they have their own particular priorities about what is and isn't *de rigueur*. At Ascot, hats, of course, are essential and, if you wish to enter an enclosure, shoulders/midriffs should be shielded from view. Trouser suits, if you must, should be full length and matching in colour and fabric. In the Stewards' Enclosure at Henley it is quite different. Shoulders can be as bare as you dare, but you'll be turned away if your hemline creeps even an inch above your knee and trousers are entirely forbidden.

If no dress code is indicated on a wedding invitation, formal daywear should be the assumption. Of course most weddings segue into evening, so many girls prefer to dress for after dark since this is when, post-formalities, they can reclaim a little attention. This is not really the occasion for the LBD, as brides are likely to take exception to funereal black, and it should go without saying that it's not your day to dress up all in white. It's fine, however, to wear black and white together, or black or white paired with a colour. Though usually not a necessity, hats can add a little *je ne sais quoi*. Obscuring the view of the bride with a wide brim won't ingratiate you, however. Hats should be taken off before you eat.

Smart casual is the most prosaic dress code and an oxymoron for most, to whom things are either smart or casual. This concept surely only comes easily to dress-down Chino-ed bankers. That said, it's not an uncomfortable state and it is simple enough to muster something up from your own wardrobe. Essentially it requires an effort that's smarter than usual. This is the time for clothes brushes, neat pressing, all buttons present and correct and any toothpaste dribbles, scuffs and rips banished.

It is the overall balance that is key. Temper sparkle with something more downbeat, or dress up a relaxed outfit with tastefully glitzy accessories. A cute frock, on or around the knee, can only please onlookers. Certain blacklisted items will jeopardise the chances of a re-invite; avoid trainers and sportswear entirely. Jeans' suitability is debatable as a more mature party demographic is likely to frown at denim, but in more metropolitan circles, smarter designer jeans worn with heels and an evening top is quite the conservative uniform.

Subjectivity is at its highest here, so weigh up the evidence (the venue, the occasion, the guests) to ascertain the precise ratio of smart to casual. Dress to honour the occasion. For theatre, opera or ballet, dressing up can make the evening more memorable. Think about the timing of the event and wherever it may be that your chaperone is treating you to dinner. For first nights, or if you have top-notch seats/box, heels and a cocktail frock wouldn't be overdoing it. Matinee performances are more relaxed. It may seem wrong to dress up for a mid-afternoon performance, but remember that you will emerge in time for the evening's activities. Zero effort shows zero manners.

Food and Drink

Table Manners

There is such a thing as overdoing it. Perfect manners should not stand out like finishing-school finesse. They must be subtle and natural; basic courtesy and sociability will be rewarded with return invitations. Manners are not only due at dinner parties and restaurants, but should extend to everyday picnics and barbecues. Familiarity and table manners are negatively correlated, so friends are usually expected to tolerate the sight of others licking fingers and elbows lounging on tables.

Ragdoll posture must be saved for the beanbag; sit up straight. Touching up make-up should never be done at the table (and must remain a secret of the boudoir). Mobiles must be silenced and never placed on the table. Staring at your neighbours and any fidgeting (i.e. taking candle wax impressions or shredding place cards) should have been long outgrown.

Grabbing at food is so animal. Put others first, so pass things around, hold dishes and help serve. Don't take huge portions (you'll be sorry if it tastes awful) or the last of anything. Top and tail requests with pleasantries. It might seem pure efficiency to jump right in and take your share of a dish when en route, but it looks so greedy. Reaching across should only be resorted to if the conduit is proving totally impenetrable. Contaminating communal dishes with your own cutlery is never on. Sauces (e.g. mustard) are put on the side of the plate; never cover your food.

Drowning food with seasoning and sauces (gravy excepted) before tasting will offend the chef and, while refusing food was once abhorred, it's much less insulting than leaving the chef's efforts looking crestfallen on the side of your plate. If none of the spread is to your taste/diet sheet, politely muddle on, or quietly find a willing donee.

The start time is a matter of great contention. Some insist on tucking into hot food (as intended), but others say that anything less than a united launch is the height of disrespect. Follow your host's lead and at the very least wait for them to sit down. Always wait with cold dishes. Starting second is never a bad look, starting (or finishing) first can be. Bread can be eaten on delivery but, as with all edibles, a graceful little pause before diving in is always advisable. All hunger-related needs must come after social duties.

Eating in public requires all private habits to be closeted. Pace yourself, so neither hoover like a wolf nor pick like a sparrow. Bring food to your mouth, rather than drop your head like a dog. Take small mouthfuls and finish each one before embarking on the next. No noisy eating (slurping, bone-crunching, chomping); no talking with your mouth full and no chewing with your mouth open. These may be the broken-record words of a school teacher, but they are still shamefully relevant. These days it's fine to delicately mop plates clean with bread (a silent compliment to the chef).

Guests are invited not only for their ability to consume, but for their talents to entertain, so don't disappoint. Try to delight your neighbours on both sides, and don't monopolise anyone. Never discuss your dieting or pick on those who are trying. Don't point out others' caveman-like manners or offbeat food choices. Whispering or sharing private jokes is a violation of the communal spirit of dining. Stifle yawns. At dinner parties, pass on your compliments to the chef without being patronising or insincere; you should only risk doing so in a restaurant if you are very well-known to them.

Handling hazards is a most fragile business. A foreign body in your food? If it was once (or is still) alive then the chef should know (as a discreet aside). Food dangerously undercooked? If you are sure it is dangerous to your health (i.e. chicken) and not just different to how you like it, then the chef must be (politely) told. Spillages? Spring to your feet and mop up. You should volunteer compensation where appropriate. Floss emergency? Excuse yourself; publicly picking teeth is a real turnoff. Extra vigilance is needed in the presence of poppy seeds and greens. If others are blissfully unaware of their own tooth adornments, let them know (minus the public broadcast); ditto with any messy cases of missed mouths. Fell asleep at the table? Swiftly issue apologies and generous compensation (gift, flowers). Never deny the hangover.

Table Settings

The sight of a dining table decked out with monogrammed family silver for an eight-course banquet will make most miscreants attempt the tablecloth trick – all that clutter, all those rules. Equally, the spectacle of pomp can give a kick to those more accustomed to snacking on the sofa. Table accoutrements are a function of formality and tradition and, for that, rather outdated.

Cutlery management should really be about preventing food flying across a room, but social order has imposed its own rules on knife and fork usage. Correctly, they should be held with the handle tucked into the palm, thumb down one side of the handle and index finger along the top (but the novice holds a knife like a pen and shovels her fork like a spade, all with fists furled). If solely using a fork, it's okay to hold it with prongs facing upwards. Scoop up soup by pushing the spoon away from you and, when rounding up the dregs, tip the bowl away from you.

Resting your cutlery on your plate between every few bites is an effective pacer (slow is better than fast, but not too slow). Soup spoons are generally considered too big to be put into the mouth whole (eat off the side); eating from/licking a knife is a solecism of the highest order. When you have finished what's on your plate, rest your cutlery in the six o'clock position (or at least with handles facing south).

Those bamboozling place settings are really very simple – just start on the outside and work your way in. If you are in any doubt, hang back and watch the others. Forks go on the left, knives and spoons on the right and pudding tools above the place setting (or delivered fresh post-main course). There may be a bread knife on/near the side plate to the left of the place setting.

Like cutlery, the more grandiose the event, the more numerous the glasses. Normally, you can expect at least three, all crowded together in the top right of the place setting. There'll be a larger bowled glass for red wine, a narrower one for white wine, one for water and, sometimes, a champagne flute. It's fine to arrive at the table with your aperitif, but finish it and have it removed at the earliest convenience.

A side plate signifies bread issues. Chunks should be torn off rather than the whole roll bitten into (or cut), and each morsel buttered separately. Butter should be stationed on the plate before being spread using the knife supplied

with the side plate. In the absence of a bread plate, use the side of the dinner plate or, in informal or rustic settings, the table will do.

The key to polite napkin conduct is to minimise exhibition. Consign it to your lap as soon as you sit down. Affect a delicate blot, not a 'wax-on, wax-off' wipe. Never use it to blow your nose. If you leave the table during the meal, leave it on your chair; scrunch up and leave by your place setting at the end of the meal. A napkin tucked into your collar suggests a mess is anticipated and, therefore, that you have bad table manners. Napkins folded into creative shapes, napkins offered in wine glasses and napkin rings are horribly passé; to play it safe, fold simply and use freshly laundered linen (not paper) for formal or impressionable occasions.

Canapés

Are canapés a conspiracy invented by resentful caterers? What other possible explanation can there be for something so eternally unmanageable? Why must appetizers be so unwieldy? Imagine the hilarity back in the kitchens as hotshots and bigwigs are incapacitated by gob-stopping vol-au-vents or humiliated as their cherry tomato spurts into the eye of an important associate.

Not only is the canapé itself so very problematic, there's the added anxiety of not knowing when the next crumb is going to arrive if you are starving and getting progressively tipsy on an empty stomach (endless champagne top-ups and huge delays between delivery are surely part of the plot). Since it's such an old trick, the practised and forward-thinking might prefer to (sensibly) eat in advance.

The perfect canapé is small enough to be easily consumed in one mouthful without dislodging one's lipstick. Those with the most petite of portals should make a decisive dissection rather than nibble round the edges like a squirrel. One small blessing of canapé culture is that anything too bulky and unladylike can be declined. Besides, it doesn't do to accept everything offered to you.

Bide your time. Don't ingest if you think you're about to be introduced to someone. The safest time to consume is when feeding time strikes the entire well-settled group.

Taking two canapés at a time isn't a good look, no matter how hungry you are. Double-dipping a crudité back into the sauce is as offensive. If ravenous (and if possible), have a tactical supper by piling up a plate and surreptitiously taking it into a quiet corner. This saves obsessing about the next consignment and having to shrewdly chase waiters around the room.

Some canapés are hell to publicly handle. Tip: avoid eating and avoid serving. Never attempt smoked salmon if it requires more than one mouthful. This slippery fish is impossible to tear in half with teeth. King prawns have a shell to battle with, a tail to hide in a flowerpot and then leave fishy fingers. Satay sticks require primal gnawing after the first bite; dispose of the stick on an empty tray or, if required to be extremely polite, jettison in the Ladies (demeaning and inconvenient). Always eat cherry tomatoes with mouth firmly clamped shut. Spitting out an olive pip in public, even if delicately executed, just cannot be done formally.

Messy Foods

Vegetables

Peas should be speared on to the top of a fork (prongs facing south) and then a few more squashed on with a knife. Don't elbow neighbours by scooping up peas with an upturned fork. In more casual company, an upturned scoop is perfectly acceptable.

Globe artichokes are painstaking with questionable rewards. Peel off a leaf, hold by the pointy tip, dip in the butter/sauce, scrape off the pulp with your bottom teeth and discard the rest of the leaf. Repeat until you reach the tiddlers nearest the choke. Cast these and the white hairy beard aside and eat the choke with a knife and fork.

Eat asparagus spears with fingers, unless covered in messy sauce (leave any woody ends). Pick up by the bud-free end. If they are an accompaniment to a main dish, eat with cutlery.

Animals

Cut wings/legs off small birds using a knife and fork. Picking up the body is considered awfully coarse, though the limbs can be delicately handled.

Spare ribs and chicken wings are shameless finger food (and, inevitably, face food), demanding an animalistic approach with napkins on standby.

Big mouthfuls and a firm grip are essential for keeping burgers intact. If defeated, remove a layer. Only use cutlery as a last resort. (N.B. officially, sandwiches should be held with one hand and put down in between bites.)

Snails are slippery blighters. Hold tongs in one hand, and special snail-spear in the other to procure the flesh. Slurping up the garlicky, buttery chaser from the empty shell is most improper in stricter settings – sopping it up with bread is a little better.

Cheese

Respect the original shape. Cut round cheeses like a cake (triangular slices). With triangular wedges, cut off slivers parallel to the length (never cut off the tip or through the length). With Stilton, purists prefer to use a spoon to scoop out from the middle; alternatively cut off a wedge. Cheese should be eaten in mouthful sized portions; break off a small piece of biscuit, add a morsel of cheese, and eat in one. Consume any rind you care for.

Melted stringy cheese has a mind of its own. It's best to give in and embrace the tangle (French soup, pizza, gratins).

Eat pizza with cutlery when you are on show; takeaways are informal and can be eaten with fingers. Tip: bend the crust corners upwards and towards each other to prevent topping from sliding off. Support end with other hand.

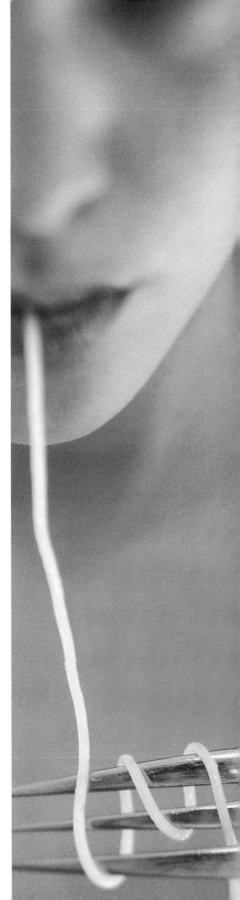

Prongs

Corn on the cob is the messiest food of all. Buttery faces and fingers require a proper clean up and teeth a serious floss job afterwards. Utilise cob forks and keep bites small. Clean up in the Ladies (not at the table).

Dive fork vertically into spaghetti and twist until a neat and manageable mouthful-sized bundle forms. Any stray strands should be elegantly bitten off, not slurped up. Watch out for pasta sauce splashback on your chin, clothes and fellow diners.

Squidgy cake should be eaten with a fork in company. In private, enjoy the primal hand-to-mouth pleasure.

Fondue rules: don't steal others' sticks, don't oust others' efforts, don't forget about your own. Those who fail and drop their bread/meat in the pot must declare their blunder.

Offending Articles

Cherry stones, olive pips, bone, gristle. Anything that requires expulsion from the mouth should not be bailed out with fingers. Instead, discreetly spit it into a cupped hand and then deposit on the side of your plate.

Bones are generally the preserve of dogs, so it will always be controversial for humans to scratch around for that hard-to-access nutrition. Don't gnaw on any kind of bone matter in uncertain or formal situations; smooth any furrows if your dining companion chooses to let nothing go to waste.

Everyone knows not to drink the finger bowl (don't they?). Essential for in situ clean ups, apply common sense and a delicate touch. Daintily dip one hand at a time, fingers only, and be careful not to spill the water. Pat hands dry with your napkin.

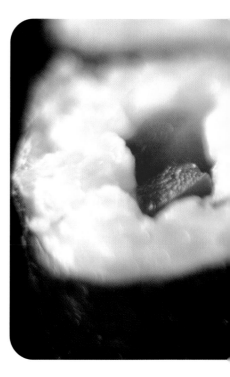

Sushi

Every stage of the sushi ritual is bound by custom and, since it's not a home-grown doctrine, it would be churlish to defy it. Rest assured that applying some basic principles will enhance your sushi experience. It is unlikely that a breach in custom will bring head shaking from the average onlooker, but self-appointed Western connoisseurs are often less diplomatic in their disapproval (despite bastardising many of those customs).

Practise with chopsticks at home if you are over the age of 16 and inept. Hold both sticks parallel in one hand, midway down their length. Your middle finger rests between the two sticks, and thumb and forefinger hold the top one. Keep the bottom stick still and pincer with the top stick. Never use chopsticks as pointing implements or to pass food around; always offer from a plate. Ask

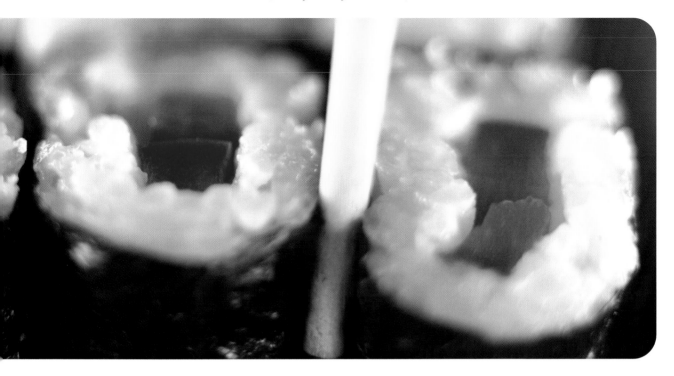

for a fork if the alternative means going hungry. Unless you're in the rawest of restaurants, don't rub your chopsticks together to remove splinters; it's rude, unnecessary and insinuates that their chopsticks are cheap.

Beginners can stick to sushi, which can be eaten with both chopsticks and fingers. Sashimi (just raw fish) should be levered into the mouth with chopsticks. Sushi and sashimi are ordered from the sushi chef or appropriated from the conveyor belt; drinks, soup and other foods are ordered from waiting staff.

Pour soy sauce into the saucer (it's polite to pour out soy for your dining companions) and mix in some wasabi to taste. Don't add too much as it's hot like strong mustard. Then, fish facing downwards, dip sushi into the sauce. A direct hit of soy or wasabi onto sushi or sashimi, or leaving sushi to soak in soy, looks amateurish and might raise a few eyebrows, although it is commonplace. Pickled ginger is a palate-cleanser, not a garnish. Eat a slice (with chopsticks) between different types of sushi.

Drink miso soup straight from the bowl and eat the bits with chopsticks. Have as a starter or, as the Japanese do, during the meal. It's known to work as a hangover cure.

Sushi rolls and nigiri (the rice-based sushi with a fish topping) are served in pairs (symbolising husband and wife). Sashimi is served in sets of three and it's good form to offer the 'mistress' to your consort.

Sushi should land in the mouth fish-side down for maximum tastiness (your tongue warms the fish so you won't just taste the rice) and should be consumed all in one. This is almost impossible without overloading; bite in two but, in less familiar company, don't chance a messy collapse.

Profligate over-ordering and food wasting is abhorrent to Japanese (or your dining companions') sensibilities. In conveyor belt bars, the never-ending loop of temptation can be distracting. Keep one step ahead and grab when you see what you fancy (condensation in the lids indicates freshness). Stock up and employ imaginary blinkers.

Wash it down with beer, green tea or sake (tea and sake should be poured communally). Placing your chopsticks on the soy saucer parallel to the sushi bar signifies game over. Tell the sushi chef when you are done (if you think he'll be interested), but the bill should be summoned from the waitress.

Seafood

Shells and Bones

Fish on the bone is a labour-intensive procedure rife with social rules; avoid in exacting circumstances. Traditionalists start at the head of the fish and work down the spine, on one side and then the other. Nothing larger than smallish mouthful-sized pieces should be eased off the fish. Flipping the fish over to get to the underside will most likely result in being struck off the social register. Instead, the bone should be lifted up and flesh from underneath eased out. Of course, some believe that such rules are irrelevant, so rebel at your own risk. Going for the head or tail is bestial by anyone's standards, so always leave intact. Bones will continuously present themselves in your mouth; extract in a delicate fuss-free manner. It is a bit of a palaver – order a fillet (or waiting staff will offer to take it off the bone for you in better restaurants) when it matters.

Start attacking shell-on prawns by topping and tailing. Then peel off the shell by starting at the 'seam' where the legs meet the underbelly, and remove the black veiny string along the spine. Never attempt out of reach of a finger bowl. If naked but for the tail, pick it up by that to eat, and discard (onto your plate, of course).

The mode for *moules et frites* is to use an empty mussel shell as a pincer; one hand holding a plump mussel, the other hand pincering and delivering to the mouth. More uptight types prefer to use a fork instead. Gather empties in the bowl provided.

Oysters

Aphrodisiacal? Most likely because a woman who can be persuaded to eat a raw oyster will most likely do anything. Oyster virgins must prepare for what is an acquired taste. A platter of oysters is often shared; it's uncivil not to try, but fine to abstain knowingly.

Take the oyster (in its shell) by the hand and squeeze some lemon on to it. Give it a delicate shake to check that it has been detached. The restaurant should have done this, otherwise use the oyster fork (found to the right of your plate) to loosen. Some prefer to take aim with the hinged end facing towards the mouth as this narrower end serves as a funnel for the juices. Others prefer the more open and flat end; argue it out amongst yourselves. With your head tipped slightly back, mouth expectant, carefully slide it in. Do not chew. Hold it in the mouth for a second to savour it and then let it slide down the throat. Farmed oysters should be grit-free, but occasionally a piece of shell shrapnel will come along for the ride; delicately remove. If it's all too caveman for you, use the oyster fork, but never attempt to cut one up.

Oysters are not the stuff of cheap dates so, unless you are a truly faithful fan, don't order them. In addition, they are also best washed down with some champagne (or, failing that, crisp white wine). The oyster aficionado knows to only order them in the months which contain the letter R, when the sea is at its coldest.

Caviar

There is no escaping accusations of ostentatiousness when ordering caviar. It's a useful accessory if you're nurturing a diva reputation, but know your facts and impress your adoring audience. So, caviar is the roe of the sturgeon fish found in the Caspian Sea. The average portion is about 30g, so binge-eating caviar is out of the question (and would be most grotesque).

Using the serving spoon, dollop a modest quantity onto your plate. Never overload the spoon and never drop a single egg. You should use the back of your hand to taste caviar – the fleshy part between thumb and index finger. This can appear pretentious, so play it down amongst more straightforward company. You can earnestly argue that you're testing for freshness (off caviar will smell on contact with skin), but only attempt if you have total belief in your caviar skills. Caviar should never taste salty – if it does it isn't fresh as salt has been added to preserve it.

Purists will eat caviar as simply as possible; accompaniments such as sour cream and onions are unsophisticated as they mask the true taste. Russian vodka and champagne are obvious accessories; you can consume in large quantities as the oil in caviar lines the stomach.

Once opened, remove the caviar from the tin and store in a champagne flute. Keep it cool; always serve at room temperature. Caviar is good for you – it contains vitamins A, B, C and D.

Lobster

Lobster, a large clawed crustacean, is effectively the armoured tank of the water world. Some heavy-duty kit and a dedicated performance are required to extricate flesh from the tail, claws, legs and body. Approach the process slowly and carefully to reap maximum return for all your efforts and minimise mess. There is a standardised order to the procedure, which any girl with social aspirations should understand.

Some restaurants edit the lobster down to just the tail and claws, while others serve it whole. The weak of will (and prima donnas) can ask the kitchen to prepare theirs without accruing too much shame. Such a request may be silently dismissed as defeatist amongst certain company, however, and you will miss out on a rare excuse to play with your food. Lobster thermidor – when the white meat is extracted, cooked in cream sauce, stuffed back into its shell, sprinkled with cheese and finished off under the grill – is an excellent choice for those too ashamed to ask for help or too posh to poke.

Most restaurants serve lobster in an open shell, promising instant tail-meat gratification – the biggest and arguably the best bit. As with most things in life, when starting to eat a lobster, always pick the low-hanging fruits first – in this case, that's the tail and claws. Anything remaining is usually the territory of the highly experienced, ambitious or those who like to show off their anatomical knowledge of a lobster.

Using a knife and fork, begin with the tail-meat. The claws will often come ready cracked but, if not, there will be special lobster crackers supplied. Use as you would nutcrackers, taking care not to damage the meat inside. Bend back the 'thumbs' from the larger part and, with the lobster fork, pick out the meat (remove or ignore the cartilage). Then pick out the large chunk of meat in the bigger half of the claw, using the crackers to open them up further if necessary.

Still hungry? More delights await you in the form of the green-coloured tomalley (liver) and, in lady lobsters, the pink-coloured coral (roe). These require an intrepid determination. Legs can be twisted off and, in casual company, the meat gracefully sucked out.

Footnote: girls should know that lobsters are cooked alive because the flesh deteriorates very quickly once they are killed. Whether they feel pain is a fiercely debated issue.

Wine Principles

What a rarefied world has evolved from a bunch of grapes left to rot. Many of its commandments may be purpose-driven, but many are pure unashamed snobbery. By playing the buff, you risk appearing a certain (unattractive) social stereotype. What's more, a buff easily segues into a bore, so unless you are amongst oenophiles, don't regale your company with wine-talk. Much better to quietly look the pro and command plentiful respect.

Choosing a wine without looking like a complete idiot is a question of dissertation-league complexity. There are no safe bet grapes and, while there are cheap gems, the fretful should aim for something tried, tested and a little more expensive. Price won't guarantee quality, but a few extra pounds could make all the difference.

Matching wine to food is, in theory, the theme – white for light foods and red for richer foods – though there are some exceptions and there is free will. It is acceptable to drink what you like; to criticise is far ruder. Rosé is often a good compromise and food-matching fanatics can always buy by the glass. Mixing wines is acceptable. The order imposed by traditionalists is dry before sweet, light before heavy, young before old and white before red. Needless to say, this is open to modern debate and personal taste.

If the wine list is like a telephone directory, summon the sommelier. Do not be ashamed to order house wines in respectable establishments as they are carefully selected to reflect the quality of the restaurant (dates may be impressed by such canny economics).

Allocate at least half a bottle per non-driving person. If you can't pronounce the wine, confidently order by the bin number, or casually point at it on the list. Commit your order to memory to ensure recognition upon tasting.

Scoffing at screw tops signals wine ignorance. No longer the indicators of cheap plonk, screw tops create proper closure on the bottle. Screw top wine can't be corked; tasting continues as a formality. Plastic corks, however, are the stuff of discount depots.

Investing in ever fancier corkscrews and drip collars only serves to expose the pseud. Wine kit need only be very simple: a waiter's friend (a corkscrew, bottle opener and knife in one), cloth, ice bucket and decanter (clear uncut glass with elegant curves). Just one type of wineglass per household is

generally enough. Go for something classic and reasonably sized, but avoid cut or coloured glass as this interferes with a wine's hue and clarity. Two types of glasses in the home is really quite grown-up, but can serve to enhance (or impress). Red wine glasses should be large, with a wide mouth and big bowl to release the bouquet. White wine glasses should be narrower and tulip-shaped. Giving glasses a rinse or swill out for new wine at home is fine, but always insist on fresh replacements in restaurants.

To open a bottle of wine, vertically screw the corkscrew all the way in, and then steadily (not jerkily) lever or pull it out. If the cork breaks, carefully go in for a second attempt and bless the era of screw tops. Rescue any floating cork from the glass before handing out.

Wine Behaviour

Tasting

Often the spark of awkward delegation, but no expertise is required. It's only to check that the wine is not corked (i.e. ruined by an unsound cork; loose bits of cork are not an issue), and any fool can spot a stinker. It looks murky and smells like a manky dishcloth.

First, take a sniff (but no grandiose swirling or deep inhalations) and then a small sip. Let the waiter know all is fine but, if it's obviously grim, ask the waiter to replace it. You might be presented with the cork; this is just for you to inspect the information – never smell it.

This is not an opportunity to send back a hastily chosen wine, but polite acquiescence to a bad bottle is uncool. Have confidence in your palate. Also, if the bottle needs warming up, cooling down or decanting, now is the time to ask. Don't suffer in silence.

Pouring and Drinking

The acceptability of self-administered refills depends on the company you keep and the calibre of the restaurant. Protocol demands that glasses should only be filled to halfway, without noisy sloshing. Even if no one's looking, don't fill your glass more than two-thirds full. Topping-up should never be a solitary pursuit. Some buffs hold the bottle by the indented base, but it's unnecessary and makes the bottle infinitely more wobbly and droppable.

Wine should be delicately supped and your glass put down in between sips. Avoid obsessive swilling and hold your wine glass by the stem to maintain optimum temperature (and avoid the unsavory 'Exhibit A' look, i.e. covered in your mucky fingerprints).

Footnote: Recycle your empties or the neighbours will tut and talk.

Temperatures

Wine will chill in the fridge in a couple of hours but, for instant gratification, try an ice bucket filled with cold water and ice, or a special wine jacket (freezing is frowned upon).

Reds should be served just below average room temperature (with some exceptions such as Beaujolais and hot days). Decanting looks the business and will liven up a wine; pour slowly to leave behind sediment. Leave to breathe for an hour or two before imbibing.

Serve whites chilled. Never decant; the aesthetic and practical equivalent is the ice bucket (ditto for rosé). Harmless crystal deposits and fine bubbles can be ignored, but a still wine that fizzes should be scrapped. Spritzers tread a precarious line between kitsch and travesty, and between a wise idea and a beginner's drink.

Champagne

Champagne is a drink for when only the very best will do, and all those who covet the high life shouldn't be seen to drink anything else. All fridges should have a bottle in reserve (though never feel bound to wait for an event). There are occasions when spray and show are appropriate (Grand Prix victories, yacht launches, champagne baths) but, when you're intending to drink the stuff and not appear vulgar, it must be opened unceremoniously – with not so much a pop but more of a sigh.

When shopping for champagne, the safest aim for the unrefined palate (and ample pocket) would be the big-brand entry-level offerings. Anything larger than a magnum (two bottles' worth) or a jeroboam (four bottles' worth) starts getting a bit impractical and conspicuously showy. Just for the

record, a rehoboam holds six bottles, methuselah eight, salmanazar twelve, balthazar sixteen and nebuchadnezzar twenty. The bigger the oversize, the rarer the luxury.

Before opening the bottle, ensure that no violent shaking has occurred and, of course, that it has been chilled. Peel off the foil top. With the bottle pointing away from eyes, low ceilings and priceless vases, remove the wire cage. Impatient champagne is not unknown, so keep a thumb on the cork and have champagne flutes at the ready to catch the fountain. To achieve that sought after sigh, the bottle itself (not the cork) must be twisted. Hold the cork with one hand, and grip the bottle with the other. Gently twist the bottle and the cork will ease itself out. Release the gas and hear the sigh.

Use tall, narrow flutes as the shape preserves the bubbles. Glasses should be scrupulously clean without any trace of detergent (or you'll kill the fizz). The old-fashioned champagne coupe has a certain elegance and is essential for champagne pyramids, but is poor on bubble conservation. Counteract by not letting champagne hang around in the glass for too long.

The 'correct' way to hold the bottle when pouring is with your thumb in the indentation in the bottom of the bottle and with your fingers spread around the base. Attempting this in front of more down to earth folk will summon stifled sniggers. Accidentally pouring it into someone's lap or dropping the bottle is a far worse social sin than being seen to hold the champagne bottle incorrectly. Most of us just grab it by the trunk. If

you are pouring a few glasses, put a splash into each first and then go back round and top up. This stops precious bubbles from overflowing. Don't fill the flutes more than two-thirds full. Rest the bottle in a champagne bucket filled with ice and water; have a cloth close to hand to catch drips off the bottle.

Just like wine and Martini glasses, one is supposed to hold a champagne flute by the stem to avoid warming up the contents. That said, its spindly stalk and top-heavy structure can be hard to manage with creeping intoxication (and those bubbles accelerate the process). Participating in a toast if afflicted with an insuperable aversion to champagne is an awkward situation. If compulsorily provided with the offending substance, just raise your glass and redistribute post-toast.

Spirits

Spirits are not free from the dogma of expertise; pour a blended whisky on the rocks for an aficionado and await their withering censure. Bluffers are safest spending more than less; settling for no-frill cheap brands is almost as distasteful as swigging out of a bottle.

Traditional rules have been diluted by fashion and the socially vain, so take them or leave them. Whisky should be served in a heavy-bottomed tumbler with an accompanying small jug of still, room temperature water. It should be sipped languorously. Water allows the nuances of the flavours to open up, so chilling it with ice prevents the aromas from unfolding. Ouzo, absinthe and pastis should also be served with water. Keep vodka in the freezer. Ice should be made with distilled water. Honour the quality of the bottle; save the very

best for those who will appreciate the rare offering. Cocktail paraphernalia (parasols, sparklers, fruit salads on the side) is sadly considered *de trop*.

Beyond mere drunkenness, some spirits have secondary effects – good and bad. Tequila is an upper, absinthe a mind-opener (not least for the fact that it's also high in proof; to some it's the green fairy, to others green poison), and gin a depressant (take heed if you are prone to beer tears).

Aperitifs (or before-dinner drinks) should both stimulate the appetite and awaken the palate (as well as, critically, aid sociability). A White Russian will summon disapproving sighs; an aperitif is not permitted to suppress hunger or numb taste buds. The rule is generally clear spirits over dark ones, and those on the social treadmill might like to

consider a dry Martini or non-spirits such as sherry or vermouth. If you're stuck in a mind-blank panic, stick to a classic such as gin and tonic.

Digestifs (after-dinner drinks) may not do much to aid digestion, but they are undoubtedly effective nightcaps. Usually more alcoholic than an aperitif (and usually served neat), safety shots include darker spirits such as brandy, cognac, Armagnac and whisky.

A household drinks cabinet should include a selection of glasses (Martini, highballs, tumblers) and basic cocktail making equipment (muddler, shaker, strainer). Stockpile all-purpose spirits (vodka, gin, Cointreau, bourbon, rum, whisky), essential extras (lemons, limes, Crème de Cassis, Angostura Bitters) and mixers (ginger ale, cranberry juice, orange juice, tonic water, soda water).

Day to Night

On the Move

Air Travel

To ensure that your journey passes as smoothly as possible, avoid winding up your neighbours. If you must chat, be on the alert for 'talk to the hand' signals (forced smiles, brusque responses, nose in book, earphones in). Economy class sadly involves a cruel game of musical armrests. There are never quite enough to go round. Your claims are to one and a bit only, so relinquish the bit, choose one side and stay there. Reclining your seat fully is your god-given right, but is best appropriated by lowering bit by bit in invisibly incremental stages; ensure the person behind you is not eating. Pulling yourself up by the headrest will leave the person in front of you feeling entitled to seat-reclining revenge. Don't shout across rows – passing messages via hostesses is far cuter – and never snuggle up to strangers.

Driving

Charm and a perky smile behind the wheel make for an easy ride. The rules of the road state that if someone lets you in, you should in turn let another car in (wave cheerily to thank generous drivers). Overusing the horn, cutting in on parking spaces, parking too close to other cars, rude hand gestures, queue-jumping (*sans* cheeky smile), tailgating and flashing slower drivers are all just asking for trouble in this age of rage. If you find yourself in a tussle, keep your eyes and your temper down; don't let them win by cornering you into making a dangerous mistake. If giving friends a lift home, take them to their door. The deal is you drop them off, they drop you off, no one has to sour the end of a nice journey with public transport. To induce carsickness in your passengers with daredevil driving is unkind.

Passengers and Pedestrians

Driving is the driver's issue (no backseat berating), navigation is yours. Attend to directing first, conversation second. On long trips, offer to split the driving and petrol costs. Always take care to thank your chauffeur and never criticise their car. Music choice, however, should be a joint decision. If in a short skirt, keep your knees together when getting out. In taxis, if the driver gets creative with his navigation, phrase your superior knowledge as a suggestion and not a command. A wronged cabbie can also be an expensive cabbie. When on foot, pavement fury is likely to arise if you stop abruptly or walk too slowly in busy thoroughfares. Be careful to adjust your umbrella height so that you don't take out others' eyes. When carrying large bags, check before turning – you could take out a whole person.

Public Transport

Heed the following guidelines or face being picked on by wilful school kids or flinty old bags. Let other people off first – no argy-bargy. Take up one seat only. This must also accommodate all of your personal effects. Offer your seat to those that need it more than you do, particularly anyone elderly or pregnant (N.B. pregnancy should be apparent in no uncertain terms). Don't read your neighbour's paper and be sure not to stare. Don't subject others to watching your beauty routine, rucksacks in faces, smelly foods, smelly bodies, swearing or snogging. Be aware that others may not want to listen to intimate details of your personal life, loud music through headphones, karaoke, or the recently developed nuisance of music through phone speakers. If possible, thank the driver; no one else will.

At the Gym

Coping with the unfortunate sight of sweaty, hellbent bodies engaging in a sinister ritual of self-flagellation is only ever possible with strict adherence to certain considerations. Let these small civilities slide and the situation could deteriorate to the extent that an all-out gym strike would be the only option. Sticking to these formalities, then, is a far more pleasant prospect than the thought of a world suffering an acute shortage of gym-honed bodies.

In the land of the body beautiful, it is tempting to relax into unabashed abandon. Your kit, however, should be decent (hot pants and a sports bra are not) and shoes and deodorant should always be worn. Personal music must be inaudible, mobile phones switched to silent, calls taken outside and any grunting or screaming quite positively forbidden. Mirrors are in place to check your technique, not for preening and posing. Unless you are about to save a life or prevent an injury, interfering in other people's workouts with your own I-know-best advice is unlikely to be very well received.

Competitiveness might sometimes be productive, but don't be obvious about it. Avoid staring unblinkingly at your female neighbours and never try to race them. The good news: checking men out at the gym is seen (by most) as welcome encouragement. Do use mirrors as a foil, however, and don't allow eyes to bore into them. Women may approach men, but men should be more cautious. Men are usually happier than women to receive such attention when sweating blood, but some may find the distraction an annoyance.

Time limits are often set on cardio machines – such is the obsessive temperament of the gym bunny. You exceed these at your peril. Bagsying the machines by draping your personal effects all over them looks selfish and rude. Terrorising others with menacing glares to force them to abandon their machine is anti-social. If someone has overrun their slot, the fact may have escaped them in their gym glaze. Loiter first, then ask politely. If snubbed, sneak on them to reception or just get fit on another machine. When finished, leave your machine ready to go. Even the slightest trickle of sweat should be wiped away with a towel. Putting your weights back should be seen as good exercise and not as a chore to dodge.

Nudity in the changing rooms is a fact that must be accepted. Newcomers

need to get over it and learn to avert their eyes; if you can't handle it, wash and change at home. Gym-goers who parade around like naked centrefolds are enough to put new starters off their New Year's resolutions – desist.

Hire a personal trainer and you buy into a regime. In paying for your very own boutique boot camp, you might ultimately be in charge, but all power must be relinquished to your personal trainer during workout sessions. Don't take offence when they get cross with you: this is their job. While they may be impervious to all hissy fits and whining, such behaviour is not sporting. Expect to sweat; don't expect to have fun. If you are unhappy with their training style, take time to discuss (it can take a few attempts to find the right trainer). Unsurprisingly, trainers run rigorous

businesses. Respect their cancellation and payment policies. Always do your homework or face their fury. Call if you are running late and don't expect them to extend your training past the end of the scheduled session. Wear the right kit, bring water and prepare to change your mentality.

Make a splash in yoga's still waters and you will instantly block your path to nirvana (and, more crucially, anyone else's). The simple key to yogic karma is keeping the peace. Arrive early and 'centre' yourself. Bursting in a minute before the class starts tends to trigger ripples of tension. Late arrivals should humbly position themselves at the back of the classroom. If you are over ten minutes late (five in some classes) then cut your losses; the sense of disgrace won't be worth it. Sensory overloads

also pollute the vibe. Banish all auras of perfume and fags. Outdoor shoes are rarely invited to the party. Follow the majority and go barefoot or wear soft socks (but beware of slippery mats).

Any socialising must be conducted under your breath, but never during tuition. If your phone rings, punishment is instant. You must grab it immediately (thus admitting blame) and turn it off. If you need the loo mid-class, slip out quietly, closing the door behind you. You don't need to ask first, but your absence will be noted if nature always calls at your most dreaded pose. If the poses are too hard, muddle along with a diluted position. Leaving before the end of savasana is considered the height of rudeness, and in yoga land, rudeness obstructs personal peace. Manners are key for your own progress.

Salons and Spas

For some, all it takes to relax is to drop all clothes to the floor. For others, the mortification of potentially landing a male therapist or of having a bosom pummelled by a stranger is more likely to leave their muscles in an almighty knot. The key to flat-out relaxation is to take charge. Learn to say what you do and don't want – forking out to unwind buys you that right.

Hurtling into an appointment is like head-banging into a ballet class. Arrive in the right frame of mind by ensuring that you are there 15 minutes ahead of time. Ease into the zone and slip into your robe. Remove all jewellery. Don't store this in your robe pockets; you are likely to be too absent-minded post-treatment to remember to reclaim it. Switch off your mobile and speak only in hushed tones in public areas. If this is your first visit to a particular spa, you will complete a consultation form. Now is the time to state any aversions (e.g. male masseurs). Good spas offer free services such as steam rooms, saunas and pools alongside treatments. Ask for a tour to discover what's included, arrive even earlier to make the most of facilities. Activities that involve getting wet are best done before treatments. If you are late, expect your treatment to be shortened. Disruption (of schedules or serenity) will be sniffed at.

Wear what makes you comfortable, be it a swimsuit, bikini or towel. Be sure always to sit on your towel when in the sauna. Remain demurely robed when padding about between facilities. Most spas require you to shower ahead of using pools and hot tubs. Wearing the disposable slippers provided by some spas is more glamorous than receiving a ticking off for not doing so.

Worrying is unacceptable in a spa. The body-shy should take comfort in the fact that therapists will have seen many bodies more unsightly than theirs. Therapists may be alarmed by excessive hairiness and bad hygiene, however, so good grooming is only polite. Masseurs are often trained in the 'art of draping'. They will leave the room and allow you to undress and position yourself under a sheet. During the massage, only the necessary body part is exposed, leaving the rest concealed. When finished, the therapist leaves the room again for you to dress. You can keep your pants on, of course, or ask for some disposables that won't be ruined by the massage oils. There is no obligation to keep your pants on with male therapists; dealing

with nudity is their problem. If shy, you might prefer reflexology (feet only) but would be best advised to steer clear of hydrotherapy (it requires full denuding).

It is easy to cast off all control when under the spell of relaxation, but do try to remember that therapists should be steered into enhancing your pleasures. If the dolphin music is starting to grate, if the temperature is too much, if the pressure is too feeble, just say so. Small talk is superfluous in spas. Therapists will follow your lead in conversation so if you have questions, ask away.

Once the treatment is over you will be told to 'take your time in getting up'. This doesn't mean go right ahead and doze off – though it may be your inclination at this stage. Instead, stretch and breathe and don't give yourself a head rush leaping off the bed.

The beauty treatment most likely to cause palpitations is the bikini wax. Nerves can be soothed by booking in with a good salon – you won't regret the extra cost – and making sure that there is enough hair there to wax (grow for six to eight weeks beforehand). Be sure to avoid sunbeds before and hot baths afterwards. For Brazilians (landing strip) or beyond, the knickers will have to go and you will be asked to contort yourself into a number of strange and intimate positions. Your therapist will already have seen at least 20 bottoms up in the air that day, so relax.

Wear open-toed shoes when having a pedicure, to give the polish a chance to dry. Always pay for manicures in advance to avoid smudging wet nails when diving into your purse. Set a few coins aside for a 10 per cent tip.

Paying Your Way

Spending money does not seem to be a problem, but handling it well is quite another matter. Money is taboo to talk about but forever on our minds. With envy and greed lurking in the shadows, *faux pas* and effrontery are never far away. The single ugliest solecism may be stinginess, but a great many follow close behind.

Discussing money is vulgar. The cardinal rules of money talk can't be overstated. Never ask what someone's salary is, the price of their house, the value of their inheritance or the cost of any expensive-looking possession. Do not mention your own assets (except to your closest confidant). Rules can only be broken with known peacocks. Some may enjoy the ego trip and novelty of telling, but steer well clear if in doubt. N.B. if you have to ask, ask indirectly – 'was it expensive?' rather than 'how much?'. If you are asked the same and are happy to divulge, then do so with a cushion of coyness and humour, never smugness or solemnity. If you find this too intrusive, just tell them, wryly, that you couldn't possibly say. It is rather more acceptable to talk of poverty than plenitude but to drone on is just a waste of conversation.

Since meanness is so unattractive, be sure to give more than you take (it may be easy to forget what you owe to friends, but they won't). If mingling with the moneyed, it is up to you to excuse yourself if struggling to stay afloat. Any freeloading is quickly begrudged, while

becoming bankrupt by living a fantasy is very disturbed. If someone insists on treating you (e.g. to a weekend away) return the sentiment by buying smaller treats along the way.

Not only is throwing money about insensitive, but it will bring out all those who are eager to separate you from it. If new to money, it is better to act like you've had it forever. If you are at the northern end of the salary scale, have some respect for the southerners. If you are eating out together, then pick somewhere that you can both afford. Get to grips with *noblesse oblige*. If expecting your not-for-profit/student friends to dine on Kobe beef with you, you should offer to pick up the bill. Attempt neither to sound patronising nor appear profligate. Extravagance can be a valid indulgence once in a while. Make it too frequent and it will begin to look quite horribly flash.

Lending and borrowing can both create very sticky situations. One side always takes the transaction far less seriously than the other. Both are best avoided among friends. Of course, if a good friend has lost their purse and is marooned without money, it's your duty to loan. If they are in longer-term debt however, it is better to keep friendships pure from the messiness of money. Put more simply, someone might never see their money again. The general rule is only to lend out what you don't mind losing forever. Avoid having to borrow small amounts by always carrying cash.

While it's so much more agreeable not to bother counting small debts and to assume that all will balance out in the end, this should only be applied to your loans and not your debts. When someone has paid for you, they should be reimbursed as soon as possible; the amnesiac should probably make a note. Don't let it get to the stage where they have to ask twice – it's uncomfortable for them and will feel like a slap on the wrist for you. If awaiting payment from someone else, it's perfectly acceptable to ask for it; some people do require more pestering.

Moving debts beyond the monetary realm can be much more civilised. If a friend buys you your cinema ticket, say, trade it for a return trip. Likewise, if a favour (such as baby-sitting or offering accommodation) has been performed by a friend to whom giving money may feel inappropriate, consider payback by a gift of the same value.

When it comes to tipping, obedient customers leave a trail of coins behind them regardless; dissidents refuse to subsidise criminally low wages when they've already forked out; the shy are unwilling to imply others' subservience; those who only carry plastic guiltily shuffle off. In fact, leaving a tip should depend solely on whether you've received good service. To dump all the shrapnel from your purse, or make calculations down to a half-per cent is just not in the spirit of gratitude – if anything (as always), think generous.

Restaurant Behaviour

There's a price to pay for having your dinner cooked for you (apart from the bill, that is): the price of being out and on show in the community. For some, seeing and being seen is the attraction, but a public persona must always be assumed as watchful eyes and ears are all around. Poise and presentation are paramount; hunger strops and food fights are for the foolhardy.

Restaurants are judgemental places and are disappointingly prone to being impressed by power (it's always clever economics to favour the high rollers). Pigeonholing starts with the phone call. Perhaps you'd like the best table? Ask them to suggest the nicest but never demand it. Unless you wield genuine power, any demand is unlikely to elicit the response you desire. Instead, if you suggest that this is a special occasion,

then many will oblige you with a few privileges. If you prefer no fuss then keep your approach low-key. As any gastronome knows, you should always book. There is no point leaving it to chance, especially on weekends. Very sceney restaurants tend to butter up the better-dressed. Those who dress like big spenders can often be kindly rewarded with better service.

Appointment-keeping is obligatory when dining out. Call ahead if you are more than 15 minutes late. As the host you should aim to arrive slightly early. Host duties also include making the booking and giving guests a free rein to select the priciest options; their part of the deal is to choose modestly. Angling for the best seat with the best view will require delicate manoeuvring. If faced with table position envy, bag

the best spot by attaching yourself to a well placed person under the ruse of increasing sociability. Superiors have rights to the best seats, but traditionally girls should also be offered them. Resist grabbing the chair from waiters as they goad you into your seat; stand until you feel the chair on the back of your knees and then begin to sit. Don't forget to thank them. It's almost compulsory not to have made your choice before your waiter comes to take your order, and is far more important to settle in with your dining companions, so opt for those 'couple of extra minutes'.

Once you have chosen, close the menu (the universal sign that a Decision Has Been Made). If a waiter then fails to materialise it's time to deploy the subtle art of catching an eye: raise an eyebrow, lift the chin and elevate your posture.

Failing that (a couple of attempts may be required), try a small hand gesture or a subtle 'excuse me' when the waiter is in range (say it with a smile and they won't be hurt). Never shout, click your fingers or whistle. Dismissing the waiter is no more than a cheap trick for self-aggrandisement. When asking, always say 'please' and when receiving, 'thank you'. Taking a softly-softly approach is the best tactic when your dinner is in others' hands.

Opting out of eating always seems rather antisocial; to then scavenge off others' plates is simply cheap. Group diners should agree on the number of courses before ordering. If you are the only one to have a starter then you will appear self-absorbed. If alarmed by the potential calorific input of the meals on offer it's fine (and can be fun) to order two starters. If the menu is *sans* prices, forsake the showiest dishes. Whatever the budget, it is perfectly indecorous to over-order. Indulge any old-school boys who would feel emasculated if unable to order for the lady. Ordering a meal off-menu is venue-dependent, though smart places can be more cooperative (here, manners can make or break your chances). Food sharing and asking for doggie bags should only be witnessed by good friends. Hang around for too long after paying the bill and you risk reversing all good intentions; time is money to restaurants. If your group are determined to linger, consider ordering a further round of drinks; each round buys about 30 cheeky minutes *à table*.

How should you behave if there is a proverbial fly in your soup? Never be afraid to complain if you are seated by a stinking drain, if service is particularly sluggish, if eating implements are dirty or if your food has not been cooked to description. Ask for the problem to be rectified and don't complicate matters by losing your temper. Never shoot the messenger. If you need to send a dish back, the restaurant should always offer to keep your companion's dish warm – if not replace it – so that you can eat together. Expect to eat alone, however, if you send your food back in a group. If there are a large number of you, put off complaining unless faced with a serious problem. In situations such as these, or when someone's guest, it can be better to button your lip than create an awkward atmosphere.

If faced with a persistent problem then ask for the manager – all eyes and ears will turn, however, so keep it cool.

Paying the Bill

Those with miserly tendencies will be begrudged, those who are benevolent will be exploited; how you negotiate a restaurant bill could easily play against you. Mixing money and food takes you very close to the danger zone of mixing business and pleasure. The propensity for things to turn sour is high.

When dining in a group, quibbling over money is taboo territory. Prepare to cut your losses if you chose not to drink alcohol or have a starter; always expect to split the bill equally. On the other hand you should, of course, offer to compensate if you alone ordered a dozen oysters, caviar and cigars. It is only polite to let the designated driver off from paying full whack, though this can just open the floodgates for other needy causes – so starts the nightmare that is group bills. The situation can

become particularly prickly when the haves and have-nots dine out together. If you can't afford it, stay at home and plot your next career move. Any early deserters are best advised to leave a contribution of more (rather than less) with the person who has organised the dinner – any underestimations will only be made public in your absence. It is far better for public relations to show a little generosity at bill time.

The host (who has invited his or her fellow diners out) should expect to pay; the thoughtful soul who has merely suggested going for a meal shouldn't. Here, the group should split the bill. A host's guests should offer to contribute but the host should never accept. This is a classic ritualistic dance, necessary but purely ceremonial in spirit. It is also the host's duty to tip. When it comes to

cross-generational encounters, older guests may like to offer to pay for the host (unless they have been explicitly trumped in earnings). When dining à deux it is best for couples to take turns in paying: it is so unromantic to cleave a bill but fine for friends to split.

Always tip. Check whether a service charge is included and duly account for it otherwise. This is usually about 10 to 15 per cent in the UK and 15 to 20 per cent in the USA. Tip in cash if possible; this will improve the chance of it going to the waiting staff. If the service was surly, the tip can reflect that. If it was the food that was bad, however, it is unfair for the waiting staff to suffer. Such an issue should be taken up with the manager, who might be persuaded to knock a bit off the bill. Charm him – such perks are at his disposal.

Formal Dinners

The Set-up

The invitation lands with a thud on the doormat, the ghostly clatter of horses' hooves fades into the distance. Formal dinners, such as the ones given by the armed forces, Inns of Court and certain universities, exist entirely in the safety zone of antiquity. They can be viewed as a bewitching otherworld of arcane and eccentric rites and are, in terms of orchestration, as complex as a military operation. It can seem an intimidating prospect, but go with it. (N.B. expect no mercy for fashionable lateness.) It should be easy enough if you collect yourself and vow not to do anything too rash, and can be quite remarkably entertaining in its unusualness. If placed on the top table along with the hosts and VIPs, consider yourself well and truly arrived. The top table takes to its seats last; come prepared for stares.

Table Manners

Follow others' lead at every step, when sitting, standing, clapping, eating and bowing for grace. Never be the first to do anything – even if you think you know the drill, play safe. Since this is the world where bodily functions are deemed vulgar, it's best to make a precautionary visit to the loo before going to the table; otherwise hold out until coffee is served or make a dash for it and face the consequences. Here decorum must be ratcheted up to the top notch, so banish elbows, upturned forks and any hungry fingers. There is little point in defying the traditional rules here; solecisms are likely to be entertained with the gravity of biblical portent. Attempted anarchy will prove exhausting. Never eat in your gloves and prepare to pace yourself through a prodigious number of courses.

Toasts and Speeches

Yet more pomp is served after dinner with toasts and speeches – assume a smile and think of it as anthropology (N.B. sometimes speeches take place before dinner). The most usual toast is the Loyal Toast. This is simply the words 'The Queen!' said by the principal host, to which all must be upstanding. The National Anthem might be played first, in which case you stand for the music, leaving your champagne on the table until the music has ended. Raise it for the toast, take a sip and then sit down. Steel yourself – there is sometimes a second Loyal Toast. Speeches are usually given after the toast. You should at least pretend that the speaker has your undivided attention. Avoid any whispering or sniggering, and make sure you laugh at the jokes (some self-sacrifice may be required here).

The Port Ritual

There is some recompense for sitting through toasts and speeches: the end of the Loyal Toast signals the go-ahead for port, cigarettes and the rest of your champagne. Smokers should check with neighbours first or leave the table; never light up before the Loyal Toast. As the Establishment's peace pipe, port is circumscribed by strict – and also fabulously eccentric – laws. A port decanter is usually placed on the table so that the guests can help themselves and then pass it on. It is always passed to the left (to pass it to the right would be like rivers running backwards). With this rule in mind, if the port somehow bypasses you, never attempt an unholy change of direction. Send your glass on an express mission to the left until it catches up with the port, and hope that not too many others also missed out.

Bar Behaviour

In bars, many normal social restrictions do not apply. Here, strangers are not quite strangers. It seems that anyone who steps over the threshold will be granted special rights that allow them to approach others, and that they must likewise suspend their own claims to privacy. The bar area is the key social belt. Any girls of freakish, botherable beauty are advised to retreat to a bar's furthest reaches, while those who are socially hungry should loiter here and around any bar games (e.g. pool, table football, darts) for maximum attention. Vertical drinking is an open invitation; tables are rather more uninterruptible.

Sadly, bar life is not one big love-in. Behave in a way that is suitable to any public arena and avoid aggravating your neighbours. Adjust to the vibe rather than trying to remodel it. Don't subject people to banging jukebox numbers during Sunday lunch or drown them in boisterous drinking games or hen night hilarity; alcohol and umbrage is a nasty union. If you spill someone's drink, or your drink over their clothes, offering to fetch them another is the least you can do. If the same is done to you, however, expect no apology.

Learn to improve your bar karma. Bars are not democracies. Like waiters, bar staff have the power to decide how smoothly your evening will pass; some will happily punish and some will stoop to favouritism. Take some heart in the fact that they can be easily bribed; tip generously and you will, in theory, be rewarded with priority service. Table service should always be tipped. This is usually 10 per cent, preferably in cash, but check that a service charge hasn't already been added. A night of high-maintenance cocktails should also be rewarded; otherwise any tipping is discretionary. With pub staff, if you find that gratitude is due, offer to buy them a drink rather than flashing the cash. All orders and payment must be delivered swiftly. Umm-ers and ahh-ers face the risk of being relegated to the back of the queue. Courtesies must follow every transaction – the order, payment and delivery. Consider appropriating a bartender's name for extra privileges but don't abuse it by hollering at full volume across a packed bar.

Queueing manners are likely to deteriorate once crowding and alcohol intake increases. This is complicated by the fact that there is never any real queue, but an invisible self-regulating order. When you are faced with an hour long crush, feminine wiles (along with a tipping history) can help in advancing proceedings; waving notes, snapping fingers, tapping coins or being busy in conversation won't. Don't pose at busy bars if not waiting for service. The best non-verbal signals to get attention are a slightly pained expression followed by, on eye contact, a raised eyebrow and an expectant smile. Bar games are subject to queues too. Volunteer to double-up with boys waiting in line (but watch for possessive girlfriends).

Unless you are eschewing alcohol, it is a bruise to the communal spirit to opt out of the round. Always volunteer and never wait for pointing fingers. Unless you are putting it on expenses, or it's funded by lottery winnings (or the boss is buying), it's patronising to pay out for everyone all night. Any girls who 'forget their purses' get a bad reputation fast.

Aim for cooperative drinking, but reserve judgement on the abstemious. Don't bully non-drinkers and try to let any undrunk shots go (admittedly easier said than done when drunk). Do your best to preserve communal spirit, but don't push too hard; you may force an untimely Betty Ford confession that will mortify both parties.

You shouldn't feel you need to wait for an occasion to give a toast. If you *are* the occasion, modesty is called for; don't pick up your own glass when you are being toasted. Many people take deep offence if you avoid locking eyes when clinking glasses. Ensure that you make at least cursory eye contact with all toasting partners.

In these unfortunate drink-spiking days, what should you do if that guy whose eyes are burning into you offers to buy you a drink? Don't feel that you are in any way obliged to accept; say yes and you're officially liable to talk to him. Be wary if he has already bought it for you – if you have doubts then decline gracefully. Social butterflies who enjoy working the room should always keep their drinks in sight.

Club Culture

Getting In

The appeal of clubs can be very hard to fathom. These ego-marinated vice dens – where hearing, good vision and judgement are all compromised – are prowled by both predatory males and territorial females. Obviously the draw is in the danger, while survival is largely down to exercising a little nightclub cunning and honing the elusive skill of fine-tuning your alcohol intake. The first test is to make it through the door. Do you fit the mould? Clothes rarely get more up-and-down treatment than at the club entrance. Girls can't go too far wrong by dressing up and should yield to the club's ideology. Insouciant scruffs who are wedded to jeans and trainers are advised to check the dress code of the club first. Fine-tune your company too, steer clear of crowds; hen parties must go undercover or risk rejection.

Keeping Staff Sweet

Never, ever take on the bouncer. Girls can expect more than a little positive discrimination but the XX chromosome doesn't open every door. It's the job of the doormen to wind you up. If you are going to react here, then they assume you'll make trouble inside. Always take the philosophical high ground; never be combative, even if you are right (the door is a rights-free void). Any bouncer bribery is most unladylike. Once inside, loo attendants should always be tipped if grabbing handfuls of lollies. It's also considerate to tip a small amount on your last visit of the evening (if indeed capable). If you only visit the loo once and have an unsolicited towel stuffed into your hands, any tip you give will be generous. If the cloakroom charges, you can leave a small tip when picking up your coat, but don't feel obliged.

Dance Floor

Chain-smoking and drinking on the dance floor is a novice look that says 'I can't do this without props'. Those who take up more than their share of floor space, all flailing arms and kicking legs, will not make friends fast. The 'request pest' (who repeatedly hassles the DJ) will also never be particularly popular. By all means ask, but go with the vibe and avoid DJs in moments of pained concentration. Beware of UV lights – the adversary of anyone with dandruff on dark clothes, cosmetic dentistry, white bras or dark circles – in fact, not really much help to anyone. Finding true love here is as improbable as finding a four-leaf clover but, if a boy asks you to dance, it's painless enough to oblige for a few bars, and easy to break free as if carried away with the music. Don't look back.

Guest Lists

Just as 'premium' has come to mean 'standard-issue', the term 'guest list' has, in some clubs, become little more than a marketing tool. It can sadly come without any privileges. Generally, civilians who can put themselves on the guest list without having to exploit any connections shouldn't expect to have free entry (and not any kind of entry if arriving late). Those with friends in high places, however, may proceed straight to the other side of the velvet rope. In either case, aim for the clipboard and await further instructions – you may be ushered straight through or you may have to stand in line. Accept relegation gracefully and never pull out the 'don't you know who I am?' line. There will be a restless audience in the other queue all too ready to witness your fall from grace. Appeal quietly if desperate.

VIP Areas

If you are A-list famous and very likely to get mobbed, segregation is smart. VIP rooms can, however, be extremely overrated. All of the action and most of the atmosphere is left back in the main room. The standard of company you'll mix with will depend entirely on which 'VIPs' take up the invitation; they are often just corporate opportunists who are dull and overly impressed by the concept. Make the most of the perks, but don't look overeager. If a free bar is supplied, any rapacious consumption (and its likely consequences) will give you away as an amateur. Slip in and out and soak up the jealous glances of those on the outside of the velvet rope. Be cool and dispassionate about any real VIPs: don't stare or take photos. Pretending you've seen it all before will grant you far more VIP inclusion.

Sociable Smoking

Smoking has cachet and critics but, as a minority sport, is usually considered antisocial by the non-smoking majority. Smokers are therefore encouraged to cushion their indelicacy with suitable manners and consideration for others. This can seem perverse when smoking stands as such a totem of irreverence, and manners are most hard to maintain when social smoking is usually a result of decorum-dissolving drinking.

Thus the smoker is obliged to ask if anyone near objects to her lighting up. In someone's house, it's obligatory to ask the host first (unless another guest has already sullied the air). Smokers should perform perfunctory checks for children and pregnant women. Chain-smokers should to go outside to chug away and numb their craving; fugging out the room won't win friends.

The social smoker who only got as far as quitting buying should rotate her suppliers of freebie cigarettes, or take advantage of the icebreaking power of smoking by prioritising with strangers. If asked to donate, it is churlish (though tempting) to refuse. At work, limit your cigarette breaks as it's generally viewed by colleagues as extra time out.

Those who wish to smoke mid-meal should book in for hypnotherapy, so try to hold out until after pudding. Solo smokers should volunteer to leave the table, though generous hosts may allow them to remain.

Always use an ashtray. Flower pots, wine bottles and used plates can never constitute ashtrays. If you're in doubt, ask before making a terrible mistake, as nice-looking antique ashtrays may just be nice-looking antiques.

Elegant smoking demands that no smoke is ever seen billowing out of the nose, and that the cigarette is never left unsupported in the mouth (certainly not whilst simultaneously speaking). Smoke must be blown up and away (taking the wind direction into account). Exhaling into someone's face is novice.

All cigarette burns must be abjectly apologised for. Repress any flamboyant gesticulations or dance moves when in dense crowds. Cigars rarely do ladies any favours (and don't even consider a pipe). After all that, it's a great wonder whether smoking is worth the bother.

A note to non-smokers: neurotically waving smoke out of your way, huffing and puffing (especially outside in open air), affecting a splutter or cough and endlessly lecturing smokers really is pointless and uptight; just move away.

Elegant Drinking

Drinking is at once an ally of sociability and an enemy of manners, but getting outrageously drunk is not rude *per se*. After all, sometimes it is abstaining that is an insult to community spirit. Even with years of experience, however, it is still hard to judge quite where alcohol turns from a social lubricant into a tool for total shame.

There are largely three varieties of drunks. The cuddly drunk is prone to heart-on-sleeve confessions and subsequent over-amorous hugs turned snogs; the obnoxious drunk is prone to aggression and friendly fire; then there are those who suddenly get very 'tired and emotional', and end up crying into their half-empty glass. If prone to any of the above, go home while dignity is still intact. Don't spoil someone else's night by being hostile, needy or over-emotional. Becoming rag-doll floppy or passing out in front of others is never sexy or safe and is wholly irresponsible.

Drunkenness is driven by a cocktail of too little food and too much booze (especially when it's free). Try to see it coming. Eat well and keep knocking back the water and, of course, it's only asking for trouble to mix drinks, down shots, play drinking games or try to speed-drink with the boys. Most of us, however, are too forgetful to resist and learn the hard way. If you're obliged to conform to binge-drinking, fake those sips and don't forget that a clear spirit or mixer looks identical to a sobering booze-free straight mixer.

If a modicum of insight still remains when you've had a few, take a reality check in the bathroom. Fix your face, as a well-groomed appearance lends a mask of sobriety. Attend to your breath (alcohol does it no favours) and review the state of your eyes. If they look like they have stopped between floors, just call time.

Being befuddled whilst contained within a bar is one thing, but cruising the streets after dark bellowing cheesy chart hits will instantly transform you into a public nuisance and make you a danger to yourself. Likewise, a big group of drunks is more irritating and intimidating than the sum of its parts; don't draw attention to yourself.

The graceful drunk thinks beyond her immediate environment and goes home before it ends in tears. If events are foggy the next day, she will call a reliable friend and check for unrecalled grievous incidents and swiftly make any necessary apologies.

Special Occasions

Festival Chic

Remembering your manners after three sleep-deprived days in a field takes a little advance consideration. Within the perimeter fence, the law of the jungle is rather different. Morals are loosened, legalities are relaxed and all those who subscribe are expected to be quite the social animal. With throngs of revellers liberated from usual social inhibitions, it can be hard to think about behaviour and good self-presentation.

Each festival has its own credo, but all are governed by a unifying model of peace, unity, love and fun – more easily achieved if equipped with a carefree, sunny spirit. Moaning and complaining are permanently off-limits.

Claims on your friends are reduced and they must be permitted, without any grudge, to wander off. Expect to compromise; expect to get separated.

Strive for accountability via mobiles (bring fully charged/economise its use). Spread the love and share food, drink, umbrellas and blankets. Signing away all control to intoxication and assuming the support of loyal friends is selfish. Any amorousness should be privately exorcised in tents.

Rights to new friends are increased at festivals, so always talk to strangers. Restrain loved-up over-familiarity if icily received (an accumulative lack of sleep can affect sociability). Extend sharing to strangers and always be willing to lend a hand or tend to any casualties.

Remember where you pitched your tent and acknowledge your campsite neighbours. Extending an invitation for field punch in the tent porch to the boys-next-door may well be repaid with heroic offers to (de)construct your tent.

Late-night campsite activities – bongos, extra loud conversation, 100kW sound systems – are a complete contravention of the festival spirit. The family field is a smart strategy for neurotic sleepers, but strict restrictions apply and after-dark activity must be conducted in pin-drop silence (don't forget your torch). Expect trust to go only so far on campsites; keep all your valuables close.

Festival chic is a trial, with mercurial weather, mud and lack of mirrors all to fight against. Commit to the cause and be a bit inventive; invest in atmosphere-charging accessories. Equip yourself for all weathers; wellies with everything is fine except on scorching flip-flop days. Take note: on the grounds of taste and originality, an amnesty has been called on fairy wings and cowboy hats. Keep standards high. Bring an in-tent wash

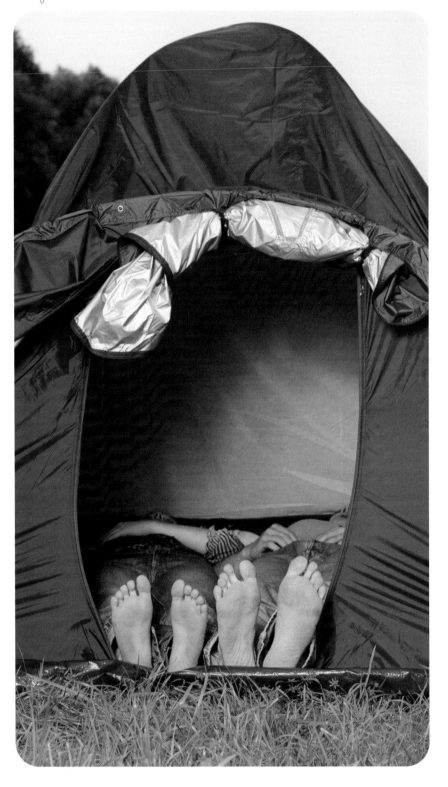

kit, waterproof mascara, sunglasses and hats for when it's game over for good hair. Essential kit should also include a robust sleeping bag, extra rug and, as excellent insurance for beauty sleep, a feather pillow, inflatable mattress, ear plugs and light-blocking eye mask.

Environmentalists and festival-goers share a few basic principles – any litter sinning will be followed by choruses of tsks and tuts. Find a bin for everything, or hold onto it until you do, and try to recycle wherever possible. Ponds, lakes and streams (and their inhabitants) like to be left in peace. Be brave and use the loos provided (remember to bring your own loo roll). Campfires, fireworks and barbecues are normally forbidden. Leave your patch of the campsite just as litter-free and nature-friendly as you discovered it.

On the Beach

Getting into a bikini is a most peculiar activity. There we are, gently sizzling like sausages, as bare as baby mice, but as comfortable as if we were in our own bedroom. Yet beyond this strange land, revealing even the tiniest peek of thigh to our own dear friends seems rather improper. It's as if being on holiday is a holiday away from our normal modesty. The fact is that some people just take the liberating effects of the sun too far. Be sure not to let the side down.

Swimsuits must look becoming, so ensure that they are neither too big nor too small. Leave the G-strings to the Brazilian glamazons; heaven forbid any transparency. Grooming should always err on the slightly-more-than-necessary side and feet should be unquestionably respectable; diving them into the sand for disguise or last-minute exfoliation is

an effete backup. Chic sunglasses must never be far away as squinting is just so ageing. Make-up should be as minimal as can be faced. Your beach towel, bag and sarong should coordinate, please onlookers and not resemble something that might have been used to carry or dry the dog.

Stay at least one towel-sized space away from the next cluster of beach-goers; don't take up too much space in high season. Don't play chicken with frisbees over your neighbours' heads or cause noise pollution with too much fun, laughter and loud music. Avoid sandstorms by shaking out towels well downwind and away from people and sandwiches. Watch the language and ribald behaviour in the vicinity of little people. Don't stare at any odd-looking bodies, though preying Adonises may

be admired with as much indiscretion as you dare. Keep sunglasses on to avoid detection.

It doesn't take much for a practised perv to come up with beaches as prime ogling grounds. Don't encourage them or offend the sensibilities of strangers by abandoning your modesty. Bikini rights are only permitted on the beach and in the water. All assets should be covered up before loping into a shop, restaurant, bar or hotel lobby. A bikini is never acceptable attire for public parks and gardens. Similarly, stripping off in public should only be undertaken with the utmost Victorian delicacy.

Only go topless if you're secluded and, even then, never be the only one baring all in your group. Girls blessed with the Body must remember that the less lucky are likely to resent excessive

preening and posing. Be careful when sitting cross-legged. This unfortunately invites the eyes in, so keep those knees firmly locked together.

Never be guarded with your supply of sun lotion, water, drinks, snacks and toys. Don't presume that someone else will take care of provisions; ask before borrowing. Aim for reciprocal altruism – you oil their back and they'll oil yours. Hot weather, warm seas and skimpy apparel can encourage couples to get steamy, but any passion on the beach should stop at kissing.

Take all your rubbish away with you, down to the very last peach stone. You must leave your patch of the beach just as you found it. Beaches and dunes are environmentally sensitive; go easy on them or face a communal glare from the whole beach.

On a Yacht

Unbroken horizons, dazzling sunsets, the sense of freedom, cocktails in the cockpit – all are implicit with a yachting invitation. The sybarite, however, might be rather less impressed to find herself rolling up her sleeves to be all hands on deck after anticipating barbecues on the sun deck, jet skis and a very large motor. Hands-off delicate ladies are therefore best advised to enquire as to what the invitation involves.

Even with the most palatial vessel, on-board dynamics are complicated by cabin fever, tight-ship rule and the preciousness of such inordinately costly equipment. Whether your host is the owner, or has just chartered for the weekend, there's usually some kind of ego on board. Boating is, after all, part sport, part exhibitionism. The best guests muck in and don't rock the boat.

Storage space is militarily minimal; capitalise the capsule wardrobe. Pack light into a squishy (collapsible) holdall with the yachting lifestyle in mind; aim chic. Boating indispensables include a sun cover-up, swimwear (more than one set), a sporty waterproof jacket, a warm top in case of chilly winds, large trophy sunglasses and clean bottomed trainers or deck shoes for use on board. Check evening plans and formalities ashore to ensure you will be suitably attired.

Before leaving terra firma, warm up those affectations of socialite glamour; the importance of perma-posing cannot be understated. You are under constant watch. Your domicile is less a floating home, more a sideshow to tourists and neighbours. Showing up your host is most ungracious; sullying the illusion of how the other half live will disappoint

the voyeurs. Save the bikini pageant for the sun deck. Don't sit on pristine suede seats when in wet bikinis and embalmed in sun creams.

'Permission to board please?' is the watery equivalent of a doorbell; it's usual and polite to ask first. The short walk up the bridge onto the boat can be quite precarious, so go carefully. Land shoes come off immediately; vertiginous heels and black soles have no place on boats, nor deck shoes on land (tar, sand and oil neuroses). Once on board, put on your deck shoes. You can brave barefoot, but mind out for any toe-stubbing obstacles. Only pedicured toes should go on show.

All boats and captains have rules, so brace yourself for a detailed rundown on alighting (frugal water usage, be tidy, stow kit in your cabin and so on). Mug up on jargon – know your port from your

starboard – and act the natural born sailor; it's part of the romance of sailing. For example, a loo on a boat is called a head and, unless you are on a big vessel with its own helipad, it's more than likely to be a limited blockage-prone service. Cue a potentially toe-curling confession; ensure you know how to work it. Check water supplies before washing your hair and keep showers brief.

The captain's word is final. On large gin palaces, however, it's quite usual for the host to hire a captain to help sail the boat. In this case the host's word is also final (never refer to the boat as a gin palace in front of your host). On larger boats (over 20 metres) there is normally a crew of some sort. Deckhands and cooks are there for your pleasure, but don't treat them as servants. It pays to be grateful and gracious.

The rumour mill inevitably goes into overdrive when ten available lovelies are cooped up together, but keep in mind that gossip transmission is dangerously efficient over water and through the thin walls of boats. In close quarters, it pays to be a nice neighbour to other guests and to other boats. When moored, only the sound of lapping waves should be heard at night and in the early morning; save music for the open seas.

Plain sailing requires considerable concentration: it isn't as straightforward as it looks. Keep out of mischief and contain your paraphernalia when the boat is being launched and docked. If you need a focus, work on pleasing onlookers. Sailing can be a dangerous and hazardous pastime, so toe the line and listen to what you are told. Help out/muck in as required. Steel yourself

for abrupt orders; pleasantries are a rare luxury when sailing. Don't snigger at the captain's docking skills – it can be difficult even for the most proficient and experienced sailor.

Good guests offer to help clear up, ensuring everything is left shipshape in recognition of the hospitality they have received. The extreme expense of yachting – the maintenance, fuel, crew, hardware, moorings, equipment, flowing champagne – should be flagged up in any guest's mind.

The crew must be tipped, via the captain, as a reflection of how long you stayed and their gallantry (your host should advise how much). On departure remember to thank all concerned. The final duty (especially if angling for a repeat invitation) is to expressly dispatch a glowing thank you letter to the host.

On a Private Jet

Welcome to life in the fast lane with no queues or crowds. Planes range from small light cabin jets to the playboy's custom-built extravaganza. The size will depend on how many passengers are on board and how far you are going.

Luggage will be stored at the back of the aircraft. Space is often limited, so avoid piling high the suitcases and aim for one (soft) bag, plus hand luggage. Avoid sky-scraping heels (cabin height is often less than human height). Favour simple sophistication over high-octane glamour and dress to fit in with your in-flight companions.

The jet set are usually driven right up to the tarmac and are only required to report for duty just before takeoff (usually 15 minutes in advance). Follow the host's instructions and don't be late; couldn't-care-less coolness won't be appreciated. Remember your passport and expect a quick baggage check.

The golden rules of the skies, unless invited otherwise, are to behave and be seated. Try to keep fear of flying calmly under wraps. The cockpit opens onto the cabin; don't distract the pilot during take-off or landing. Never be rude to, or dismissive of, the pilots, but draw the curtain across the cockpit entrance for privacy (without diva-ish dismissiveness). Solo flyers must always stay in view with it drawn back.

The bigger the wingspan, the more gourmet the feast. The larger jets have attendants (and on-board kitchens) to cater for any whim or desire, delivered on bone china with real, metal knives and forks. Sometimes you can even pre-order a dish from a favourite restaurant. Smaller light cabin aircrafts don't have attendants, so on-board supplies are there for the taking. Drinking (and smoking) are normally green-lighted but always shadow the behaviour of your host. Never consume to the point of excess, unless it would be rude not to.

Touchdown is as fabulously fuss-free as departure. The pilot will radio ahead for a car to take you from the landing strip on to the next six-star stage of your power trip. Customs is taken care of for you in advance, so landing is gloriously quick and check-free.

Before facing your public, a quick brush-down, straighten-up and once-over in a pocket mirror is advised; there are certain high-life standards to be maintained here. Leave the cabin tidy and thank your pilots. Follow up with a thank you letter and gift for your host that matches the (aspired) lifestyle.

Hotel Behaviour

'What do you think this is - a hotel?' It can be hard to know how to behave when everything is done for you and, on the other hand, what to do if it isn't. It is best to behave with charm and a touch of formality. One without the other is never as persuasive.

On arrival, check your booking - the rate, type, floor, view - to prevent any nasty surprises. Now is the time to negotiate improvements. The way you stand your ground will determine the quality of your stay. Flirting pays here. If arriving late, let them know so that your room isn't sold. If running late when checking out, a call to reception should buy you an extra hour or two (and why carry your luggage down when you can send for a bellboy?).

You are owed your full complement of stars, so if you are disappointed, say so. Do this politely but firmly, rationally and not emotionally, and at the first opportunity; never be the apologist or the pushover. If your room is not up to scratch, call the desk and ask to be shown another one immediately.

Be direct but keep an amused tone to your voice: 'I did not come to Cap d'Antibes to stare at a wall.' Any issue should first be taken up with reception, then the manager. If you are next door to hellish neighbours, never dirty your own hands (or invite repercussions); but again, leave matters to reception.

Rock'n'roll behaviour will ultimately limit your choice of hotel. Nicking the robe, the paintings, the lamps and so

on will quickly catch up with you. But entirely impeccable performances are never necessary. Eccentricities may be indulged. Unless you are as messy as a teenager, there is no need to tidy for the maid. In five star hotels you may choose to stay in *déshabille* to receive room service (in the Far East you don't need to bother to dress at all).

Hotel restaurants tend to be smart (and fairly uptight). Dress that is sub smart casual may be sniffed at. Hotel bars should keep serving until you decide to call it a night. When the bar staff start to affect weariness, take pity if you choose, but don't feel too guilty. Never trust a concierge. Their interests are often vested and their opinion is usually out of touch. Use them only as a corroborative source and for making bookings. Here you can work them like your PA and be sufficiently demanding: don't be afraid to ask for the best table at your preferred time.

The tipping guilt trip in hotels can result in considerable overuse of your wallet. If you are with a man, eyes will look to him first (it can seem nitpicking for a girl to step in here). If flying solo, yield to the guilt if the service warrants it. Tipping amounts are as follows (unit one dollar, euro or pound). Bellboys or porters: one unit per case, given as they leave your room (if overlooked in the USA, the staff will talk). Doormen: a unit if a cab is called for you (but not if ordered from the desk). As you leave for home, hand them a handsome tip

and your next visit will be a very happy one. Housekeeping: leave a banknote and a thank you note in your room (five units for short stays, more for longer). Never give it to reception - it will only be pocketed. Room service: two units for breakfast, two units for supper, one unit for drinks. The exception is in the USA where they will have added 15 per cent or 17.5 per cent delivery charge already - unless the messenger is very cute, don't bother. Managers: shouldn't be patronised by tipping.

A note on villas: don't make the mistake of treating a villa break in the same way as a stay in a hotel. Without an army of staff to satisfy your every whim, survival requires both patience and a bit of performance. To preserve your friendships, conform or cancel. Aim for majority rule - there is no pleasing all tastes (think breakfast time, cocktail o'clock, how much to spend or how naughty to be). Only ever take the best room if you're the only guest, you won it in a toss or you're paying extra.

Consider a rota for chores (but let someone else take charge as it's a grim role). Consider eating out over home cooking to avoid the inevitable kitchen sink dramas. Don't wind up other girls. Walk away from competition over boys, clothes, diets, bodies or attention. Do not rise to attention-seeking behaviour or insidious tensions. Bow to the group's sartorial consensus. Being the only bikini-ed body at breakfast will lead to accusations of self-admiration.

Perfect Picnics

Background

Be it cheese and pickle sarnies for two, or a collective effort stretched out over a long and lazy afternoon, a picnic is by definition informal. There are no laws, so it's no surprise that picnicking was a popular means of escaping the rigid rules and regime of the dinner table in Victorian times.

Whatever the scale, the increased proximity to turf is no excuse for bestial table manners. The success of the day, however, lies not only in the hands of the guests. The hostess's duties range from paying attention to detail (stylish yet practical accessories to improve the aesthetic), to taking responsibility for any rambunctiousness and practicalities such as litter (leave no trace).

So, with a little organisation, the hostess can avoid seeming as though she's two sandwiches short...

Essential Kit

Basics: large travelling rugs (one per four guests, plastic backed and no dog hairs), crockery, cutlery (never plastic) and napkins (proper/paper to match taste and class aspirations), corkscrew and bottle opener (always overlooked), solid containers for delicate foodstuffs, hamper and rubbish bags.

Domestic goddesses may like to style the set; someone is sure to bring a camera and it wouldn't do to record a garish mismatch. A cool box might spoil the aesthetic, but it saves you the crippling embarrassment of giving your guests any tummy troubles (cool box to contain fridge-dwellers such as fish, meat and dairy products).

Know your numbers and provide for all. You don't want to find yourself a fork short or your guests perching on jumpers for lack of rug space.

Hosting

Your guest list should be calculated for maximisation of fun, conversation, sporting prowess and visual pleasure. Inform guests of the proposed date, time, location and provide directions (prepare a rain contingency).

Guests should be informed of their proposed contribution. Heaven forbid that a group picnic should be a one-woman show. Split the guest list into savoury and sweet duties; strongly hint at what you'd like provided to avoid any duplications. Weed out any bad cooks and instruct them to bring drinks and golfing umbrellas (can double up as parasols). Games must be retro and suitable for the less-sporty; think French cricket, rounders, croquet or boules.

Without the martyrdom, you'll have plenty of will left to serenade guests with food, drink, comfort and fun.

Food and Drink

Those blessed with good, practical housekeeping faculties know how to pack the hamper in ordered layers, with crudités on top, savouries in the middle and, finally, pudding at the bottom.

Wise hostesses should treat guests to artisan foods; consider cheating by embellishing simpler foods (cheeses, breads) with sophisticated trimmings (pickles, relishes). Leave the lettuce at home and choose unusual salad leaves; save dressings till the final moment or risk a major wilt.

Providing easy to eat treats – finger food and ready-cut portions – makes for more delicate table manners. Tepid white wine, rosé, champagne or beer will see you summarily abandoned for the nearest pub. Use wine jackets/cool bags; on sultry days red wine should also be lightly chilled.

Formal Events

When it comes to events of the social season, stakes are high as to whose five-course alfresco luncheon or dinner party served out of the back of the Roller is indeed the best. Of course there are no actual winners, just much eyeballing, competitiveness and one-upmanship.

Table and chairs are a must for the formally dressed (especially when entertaining guests). Special touches make all the difference (starched table linens, crystal wine glasses, champagne flutes, willow picnic basket with leather accents). Provide classic British summer delicacies (asparagus, smoked salmon, strawberries), to be elegantly nibbled with minimal mess.

Optional extra: a motor capacious enough to contain the kit, with a boot that can double up as a table.

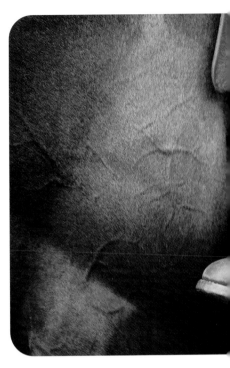

Polo

The glamourous world of polo is often viewed as a chance to buy into social exclusivity. Members' enclosures often attract fawning monarchists (after the attentions of polo-playing princes) and fortune-hunting young ladies. It's no huge surprise as, in the distance, two teams of four swashbucklers on glossy mounts – all stallion-controlling might and rippling thighs – battle it out. In this glorious, escapist world of green and pleasant lands, there's an accepted way of doing things.

The form is relatively relaxed and informal compared to other summer seasonal fixtures (the polo season runs from April–September). Spectators can either settle for grandstand seating or buy/cajole their way into the see-and-be-seen members' enclosure. The difference is a choice between eating a

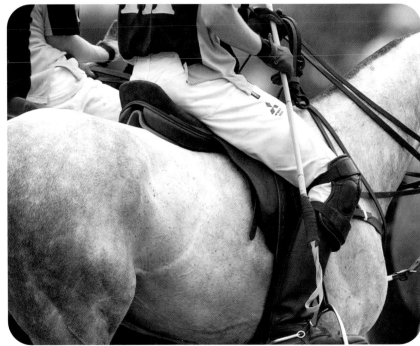

picnic on the lawn, or being presented with a lavish sit-down lunch, afternoon tea and a continuous downpour of fizz. Lunch comes first, then the polo (or, for some, a postprandial kip). Members usually watch the match from the edge of the field and avoid the proletariat in the grandstands.

Half-time (only five minutes) brings the tradition of divot stomping, where the turf kicked up by the ponies (never referred to as horses) is trodden back into place by spectators. It's a beauty parade of sorts, with a bit of silliness as spectators see quite where the effects of the champagne will take them. At very big matches, the in-crowd divot-stomp in a special fenced-off members' zone, free of the grandstand crowd.

Dress code is usually smart casual (dainty tea dresses, perhaps rivalrously slipped off the shoulder, to be worn with show-stealing sunglasses). Standards are rather smarter in members' enclosures, where a badge (of honour) permitting entry should also be worn. Shoes are of particular concern; divot stomping is the natural enemy of stiletto heels and strappy shoes, so the best thing for it is smart, flat shoes. In case of the Great British Weather, bring your wellies (very stomp-effective) and warm clothes.

Here are the rules: two quartets, or teams, thunder around a big field, three times the size of a football pitch, hitting a small white plastic ball with a mallet. Teams consist of a forward (goal striker), two midfielders and a back. The team with the most goals wins. Players wear knee-pads, helmets and team shirts with a number on the back; two mounted umpires wear striped shirts. There are goals at either end of the field and the teams change ends after each goal. The game is divided up into seven-minute periods (indicated by a hooter), called chukkas, and each game might be four, six or eight chukkas in length. At the end of a chukka there can be up to 30 seconds overtime, followed by a three-minute break. The ponies are swapped for fresh ones like new balls in tennis.

Players have a rating (handicap), that indicates their overall playing ability. A handicap can range from minus two (the worst) up to a maximum of ten. Often Argentinians have the best handicaps. Games are played where both teams' sum handicaps are weighed up against each other and the team with the lower handicap is given a few goals' lead. All very jolly hockey sticks, except that they play with mallets.

On Stage

Auditorium Order

Despite being subjected to reminders at the start of virtually every show, still the mobile rings, sweet wrappers rustle and someone chatters incessantly. A gentle reminder of the cardinal rule: the auditorium must never be treated like it is a communal living room.

We all have better things to do than waste precious minutes idling in a seat before curtain up, but cutting it fine only cuts you out – latecomers are made to wait. Arrive in good time and order any interval drinks in advance.

Disengage all phones, watch alarms and jangly bangles. Don't wear clouds of choking perfume, and avoid big hair and repetitive head movements. If you must eat sweets, decant and unwrap your ration before curtain up, or wait for a roar of laughter to drown out rustles; consume silently without slurping. Also no rummaging in handbags/nicking the opera glasses.

No talking, no canoodling and no fidgeting. No vicarious involvement, so don't shout at the baddies unless taking your little niece to a panto. Don't sing, hum or jig your body in time to the music. Don't lean forward, obscure the view of those behind you or put feet on seats. No snoring.

It's unofficially compulsory to wait for the interval before walking out, even for aisle seat dwellers. Performers are sensitive to the goings-on of the auditorium – upsetting them will just make things even worse for those too polite to leave.

Opera Specifics

Although general rules of theatre apply, a trip to the opera has its own pitfalls and particulars. Adhere carefully to bluff your way as a buff.

Opera cognoscenti can often make particularly pernickety neighbours. Any whooping, whistling or braying will have you promptly frozen out with icy stares. Feet stamping is a definite no-no. Be sure to applaud only on these following prompts: when the conductor takes to the podium (at the very beginning and after the interval), after the overture (the musical introduction before curtain-up), at the end of an act, after an impressive aria and at the final bows.

Familiarise yourself with the story (often overly-complicated and slightly ridiculous), especially if you are in the company of regulars. Surtitles provide a summary translation above the stage and can help you to keep up during the performance, but good revision will only serve to enhance *your* performance.

Impeccable behaviour is harder after soaking up the champagne at a country house opera festival, but manners must be remembered. A traditional element of the social season, the form is to don black tie (and warm layers) and luxuriate in resplendent grounds. Performances start early evening; most arrive early to soak up the atmosphere with a drink beforehand. The gourmet picnic is then eaten in the extended interval (usually 90 minutes) – bag a good scenic spot and set up camp before the evening's performance starts.

Gig-Going

All ladies must try to earn their rock credentials by getting along within the lawlessness of a gig. Within the bounds of public spirit, gigs have evolved their own code of wild, free behaviour. Be aware of others. In dense crowds, watch it with the lighters, elbow action and pogo dancing; don't throw heavy things on stage or around the audience. It'll be sticky and crowded, but even the most wayward musos always wear deodorant.

Pushing in rights depend on height, petiteness and determination, but some charm will always help to get you further forward. Smile apologetically, excuse yourself and body-swerve around other people's drinks. Stay further back to avoid sardine-like conditions and enjoy a more airy space.

Once the support acts have finished and the headline act is finally on stage, a system of musical statues operates. You should try to stay put and not move further forward, but dancing is of course permitted. Protracted conversations that are clearly audible over the music aren't usually wildly received and, unless it's a crowd cheering number, only sing along if you must. You're not the main act.

Mosh pit rules dictate that pushing others around isn't rude; this is how they dance in there. Caution is advised for the fragile, delicate or petite. Moshers are obliged to look out for and rescue anyone who's been knocked over. Never flail when crowd-surfing – keeping as straight as a board tends to earn you a longer ride.

Meeting Royalty

For some a lifelong ambition, for others more of a non-event but, for all, rules ought to be adhered to when meeting royalty. The event is governed by stand-on-ceremony etiquette (though things are lightening up a little). Rules tend to vary depending on the formality of the encounter, be it a regal summons to a garden party, or chancing upon a royal falling out of a nightclub.

On formal occasions, wait for a royal aide to present you to a member of the Royal Family; never introduce yourself. For example, 'Your Royal Highness, may I present Lucy Smith'. Now's your big moment to perform your curtsey. Just a brief bob with the weight on the front foot (men bow, obviously) – nothing too grandiose. Repeat when taking leave of them. Thrusting out a hand to shake would not amuse, but if offered a royal

hand when curtseying (or bowing), take it lightly and briefly – no bone rattling or extended shaking.

The Queen should be addressed in the first instance as 'Your Majesty' and thereafter as 'Ma'am' (to rhyme with 'jam'). All other members of the Royal Family are first addressed as 'Your Royal Highness' and thereafter as 'Ma'am' or 'Sir'. In conversation, if indeed you are permitted this far, never ever refer to a member of the Royal Family as 'you'. Instead, you should substitute with 'Your Majesty' or 'Your Royal Highness'. For example, 'I hope Your Royal Highness is enjoying this fine weather', but don't overindulge the formalities. Once upon a time it was deemed rude to dare to lead conversation with a member of the Royal Family. Things are more relaxed nowadays but your tone should be

deferential (without being bootlicking). With foreign royalty, the anxious should check with royal households in advance.

Informal situations are a little easier, but there are certain points to note. Even if down the pub, wait for an introduction rather than jumping in first, and address them as they introduce themselves. From then on, all may be at ease, but the royal in question should be led to believe the reins of conversation lie in their hands. Any fruitiness or controversial discussions should be averted unless invited. Remain low-key; over-formality will cause great embarrassment and may draw unwanted attention to the member of the Royal Family, or yourself. Take the lead from others who are obvious regular royal companions. Those who are overfamiliar are unlikely to be invited over for a cup of tea any time soon.

Meeting Celebrity

Planet celebrity is an alien world. It is a vertical community where only the truly, hugely famous are afforded a royalty status of sorts. It is also a place where all eventually take leave of usual social responsibilities. After reaching a certain level of fame and recognition, very few are inclined to condescend to humour the minions and, unlike royalty, are not obliged to either. Psycho fans and fame hags are permanently on the rampage, so any mere civilian is advised to brace themselves for nothing less welcoming than a glacial reception.

In chance spottings (especially when *en famille*), it's polite to ignore them. They're not public property and may be armed with ten-tonne bodyguards. Give a brief cheery smile if you must; don't gawp. If details really are required for recounting to friends, angle your mobile into the spy camera position but, at all face-saving costs, don't get caught.

On introduction, chat needs to be pithy and pacy – keep it in the here and now. Remember that there's no such thing as an original line; they've heard it all before. Feigning total ignorance, i.e. 'Sorry, I missed your name…', is a risky strategy known as the Long Shot. The wildly unfamiliar concept of anonymity may delight them, but you are in danger of incensing them and blowing it.

Exploit their insecurities. Butter up with (sincere) appreciation, perhaps in reference to a recent performance or award, but keep it brief. Remember, be cool, but never try to set yourself apart from celebrity gushers by criticising their work. If a celebrity encounter is chanced upon through work, assume humility, discretion and pure professionalism.

Never act rashly and greet them like a friend; we may know who they are but they don't know us. Disassociate them from any signature character and don't beg for them to perform their famous catchphrase. Avoid looking the fool and never ever remind them of any previous meetings; they won't remember you.

Avoid overfamiliarity. Steer clear of tracking them across town. The heavies will be on to you and you don't want to be taken for a psycho fan or potential stalker. Don't bring up anything that is remotely media gossip-based, personal or controversial, no matter how topical. They won't share it with you.

Remember, for the famous, there are only three options within their wonderful world: a) *noblesse oblige* – after all, they do owe their fans, b) bitch reputation, c) total reclusion.

Man Management

First Moves

If girls are to get the guys they deserve, they must be prepared to play a little romantic roulette. The more traditional approach of waiting an eternity to be swept off one's feet can become rather dispiriting. The novelty of role reversal and bold women can also be appealing to the modern man. Think of it in this way: what's the worst that can happen? The girl who is accustomed to making the first move often earns her reward, so start practising now on boys that don't matter so much. In any times of doubt, your rallying cry should be 'She Who Dares Wins'.

That's not to say it's easy, but don't be put off. Sometimes just getting to hello is a challenge. A little engineering may be called for, but smoothness is always suspicious. No one (of lasting significance) wants to feel like another notch on a bedpost. The best strategy is to work your way through a series of benchmarks. Stolen stares, the subtle approach, procuring a telephone number and then, finally, result. This may be a rather laborious process but anything more impulsive can send boys running scared. It's also a chance for you to check that they're up to the job.

Begin by unleashing a few smoke signals. Make sure that you are noticed (for the right reasons), work the 'who's that girl?' look. Establish your lair. A big noisy crowd can seem impenetrable while all-girl mobs are quite repellent. Downsize into a group of two or three if necessary. Once you are prepared to court attention (i.e. looking evidently popular and relaxed), train your sights on to your target. If he catches your eye, don't just look at your feet. Hold his gaze and smile (think bewitchingly, not inanely).

Now consider a change of scenery to allow him to approach. Both the bar and jukebox make you accessible. Go solo and busy yourself amongst cocktail menus and playlists. Don't hold your breath; you may have to approach him. If so, be decisive and do so before you lose your nerve. No cool cat would ever admit to having a repertoire of chat up lines, but with no opener there can be no start and therefore no finish. Chat is always preferable to chat up, however, so try to keep it natural, non-intrusive and upbeat. A throwaway comment about the venue or a compliment are both good options (flattery will get you everywhere). If rather more backward in coming forward, draft in some backup. A non-threatening ally, primed to drift away on cue, is useful to have to hand.

Predictably, the approach can make women appear more sexually available. Now is the time to play hard to get, so cool off or fabricate another party you have to get to. It's smart to convey your interest, however, as people are always narcissistically endeared to those that fancy them. Suggest a future encounter and then you'll need a number. Don't hold out for infinity for him to ask for yours. Sometimes boys just don't have the social skills. Taking his details puts you in control and obliges you to make the next move. If you want to see him again, you should be able to trust him with your own number. This shifts the onus onto him. A cheeky (and brief) kiss goodbye is appropriate; on his cheek close to his lips can be effective, or even on the lips if you spot the green light in his eyes.

If bothering to expose oneself by taking the initiative to call or email, it is imperative to invite a response. To say 'lovely to see you' is no invitation, but 'would be fun to meet up next week' is more like it. Invent a pretext – perhaps a work-related cause? – to save your dignity while giving you one more bite at the cherry. The drip-drip approach is a good device for damage limitation. Lure them into friendship until they can no longer resist you. Use your moles to case them out. Consider an information leak if you share any contacts, but don't give too much away.

If faced with a wall of silence, desist from drunken dialling. Resist the urge to overreact; he could be busy with a personal crisis. Or maybe he's just not interested. Allow yourself two benefit-of-the-doubt overtures (stick to email or text), and then go quietly. On the other hand, if you find it necessary to reject a first move, cushion the reality. Lies are perfectly acceptable here. Pick one of the following: you're spoken for, just getting over a messy break-up, not interested in having a relationship, not that way inclined.

Flirting

Flirting is a key that can unlock many doors – and not just to hearts. A little purr can only increase your bargaining power. This is an essential social skill that's less about what you say, more about how you say it. Play it right and this can be a delightful little game of ambiguity that is both fun to perform and fun to experience.

You will truly be flirting with danger, however, if you target forbidden fruits. These include the boyfriends of best friends and sisters and the right-hand men of your own beau. Other men are off-limits in certain situations (e.g. exes in front of new boyfriends, grooms at their own wedding). There are also a number of situations in which any type of flirting would be quite distasteful. Be wary of indulging if at a funeral or in a hospital or courtroom...

Social flirting makes the world go round, but keep your foot on the brake at all times. To the puritanical, almost any amount can be too racy. Maintain eye contact but don't prolong; slip in a quick arm squeeze but avoid lingering touches (hand-grabbing is really off-limits). Smiles and humour are requisite catalysts but, if dispensing innuendos and risqué remarks, only do so with the lightest of touches. Many men confuse playfulness with sexual desire so don't over-impose yourself (especially unwise if jealous partners and gossip mongers are lurking). Attempt to play the game, even if disconcerted by the advances being made by others. Their intentions are likely to be social, not sexual.

When it comes to romantic flirting, letting your intentions be known non-verbally – a coy smile here, an eyebrow raised there – saves much face for the unrequited. When it really matters (and it matters as, without telepathy, flirting is essential), begin by casting a long line and then slowly reel it in as they take the bait. A cursory glance over the checklist of risks is necessary before you begin. Is there a girlfriend? Is she here? Are his friends your romantic rivals?

Flirting should always be tempered to avoid any hint of desperation. It must also – if at all possible – be tuned to the target. Some men may need to be hit with a sledgehammer before they take notice, others might run for the hills if tickled with a feather. Read his signals at all times, and take the hint if only his head is facing you and his body looks like it's ready to run. Never advance to making a move unless positive signs encourage it.

First Dates

Venue

The rule (the first of many) goes that whoever has instigated the date takes charge. This involves taking care of the booking and instructions (venue, time, dress). If you have a choice, mid-week dates are best for mitigating hype. You should expect to sacrifice at least an hour and a half – have a get-out clause for dire occasions – but around three hours is average. Venues shouldn't be too low-rent or too upscale, too bland or too adventurous, or too crushingly loud or library-quiet. Activities that establish a common ground can work, but most recoil from more ambitious ideas as they don't feel normal. That tends to leave dinner or drinks *à deux* as the safe options, but monitor your intake of the latter. The biggest danger when under the influence is the optical illusion of good looks.

First Impressions

First dates are right up there with job interviews – every last breath is under the microscope. Go some way (not all, of course) to dressing for your date. If he's conventional don't intimidate, if he's downbeat, meet him midway. All men will weaken at a bit of slinkiness, but being yourself is always preferable to an act. Power hairdos or solid make-up tend to repel most people; at this proximity, a wholesome look is more adorable. Focus on your upper half as it will bear the most judgement. When you arrive, go straight in and break the ice with a peck on the cheek. A note on punctuality: your window of arrival on a first date is wafer-thin. Being 15 minutes late is just about acceptable, half an hour looks pretty arrogant. Consider arriving early to avoid that bewildered room-scanning look.

Conversation

Topics such as your biological clock, your first three marriages or your carnal history may need to be covered at some point, but now is not the time. You could ask for his potted history or a day in his life, but talk of work, family or hobbies is so textbook that to avoid it makes for more adventure. An eclectic conversation based on culture, life or the world is far more engaging. Avoid rants and hostile debates and focus on similarities not differences. Keep your swearing count down and don't bother with too much self-deprecation. He is likely to assume that it's the truth rather than modesty. If things run dry, plump for men's favourite topic – themselves. Ask predictable questions if necessary. It's unlikely he will return them so you may need to speak up to prevent things from becoming too one-sided.

Follow-up

The inviter pays the bill so, if you've been the thoroughly modern woman, it's up to you (though he may insist on paying). Going Dutch is the universal signal of disinterest. If you have been suitably impressed, take your date's arm. This is a cute, non-committal gesture that will help establish a little intimacy. If sensing his interest, the send-off is an ideal opportunity to steal a first kiss. Set this up with a silent, smiling eyelock (he should understand the invitation). Let him know if you are interested in a second date. If not, an ambiguous fudge is called for. Saying no outright is very bad form but resist making hollow promises (admittedly hard when on the wrong side of a bottle of wine). A missive the next day to thank your date is basic courtesy, regardless of how he scored out of ten.

One-Night Stands

The one-night stand (ONS) is a bit like fast food: tempting but with nauseating afterthoughts. Like junk food, it's much more of a bloke's thing and a chance for sex without the mess. In fact, there's little question that guys always want it, so going through with the act usually depends on the woman. There are, of course, many women who appreciate the value of no strings too. Quick thrills are available to anyone who gets what they want out of the situation. The tag ONS comes into play afterwards when it's realised that no further contact is desired. Take note: espresso sex with a long term romantic project may well turn it into a hit-and-run.

There are many health and safety implications. It is far safer to invite him back to yours. There's no denying that many ONSs are the result of too much

alcohol and it may sound alarmist, but the law has little sympathy for wasted girls. If you have any inkling of a bad feeling, abort. Ideally, friends should be alerted as to your whereabouts so text a close friend if you can remember.

Any dark alley gropery on the way home is just not ladylike and is bound to be viewed by an audience or CCTV. Also, don't force taxi drivers to witness any indiscretions. Once home, leave him to marvel at your record collection and superior taste in wine while you do a turbo-tidy. Conceal any embarrassing exhibits if bothered by such trifles, but if it's a true ONS, it shouldn't matter.

Regrets? It's never too late to back out by admitting a change of heart or feigning fatigue. Still all aflame? Then attend to the lighting, play some music and sit together. Slip shoes off, gently

shake out hair, nibble seductively on a cocktail cherry and chuckle at his jokes. Then stop talking and smile with your best come-to-bed eyes – intimacy will surely follow.

Once you're in the bedroom, forget all about your cleanse/tone/moisturise bedtime routine. Leave make-up intact and pyjamas in their drawer. Discuss the necessaries to avoid planting any love children/disease and you're away. It's never too soon or too late to expel him or, if at his, to make your excuses and leave. Always depart with a good reason (invented if needs be) and an apology. N.B. the less time you spend together beyond the love workshop, the more used you will feel; getting to know your conquest will lend a shred more meaning and memorability to the brief encounter.

If you're at his, the ONS is not over until the walk of shame – going home in last night's dishevelled clothes. Steel yourself for the aftermath and hold your head up high. If you wake up early, it is acceptable under the circumstances to slip out without waking him. If you are possessed of any concern for good manners, then it's imperative to leave a cute note and a good excuse, with or without your telephone number. If he is awake, try to conceal your need to be as far away from him as possible. Make your excuses and leave as promptly as you need to.

If at yours, offer him breakfast and, assuming you want no more of him, say that your mother is on her way round. Bear in mind, however, that concerted maturity and politeness will ultimately lessen your own shame.

Blind Dates

Blind dates, internet dating and speed dating must all be approached with an attitude of confident nonchalance. You have to speculate to accumulate and as love is rare and fate is fiction, hiking up your exposure will give you a greater chance of success. With luxury bespoke services currently on the rise, the old stigma attached to artificial dating is on the wane. Yet as long as social misfits lurk in this last-chance saloon of love, the stigma will never entirely go away. For the dater, your chance to ferret out the freaks might come too late, so prepare to take a gamble.

In theory, blind dates hold genuine promise. Two pre-vetted eligibles are matched by a cupid who knows both well. In reality, the miss rate far exceeds the hit rate. Success is a direct function of the matchmaker. The odds are much lower with older matchmakers (such as parents) and those who don't know you very well. Even amongst good friends, 'cute' is very subjective. Exercise your rights to grill the romance-broker and solicit a photo, but remember that it's rather churlish to refuse the efforts of well-meaning matchmakers. Once in contact, take the arranging out of the matchmaker's hands (possibly more difficult than it sounds as they are often nosy and like to remain involved). Post-date, err on the side of caution when reporting back to your mediator. If less than impressed with your date, cushion the blow – any vitriolic criticisms are likely to be taken personally.

Online dating is essentially human advertising. Your profile must be glossy and both picture and word-perfect. You are in direct competition with countless other gorgeous (and unquestionably airbrushed) delights. Only if the photo is up to scratch will the words even get a look-in. These must be full of wit and originality, and free of clichés. Excess modesty could backfire and leave you on the shelf. If you want to keep your options open, keep your profile brief with an aura of mystique. If you have exacting standards (must be over 6ft, must have a PhD, must love thrash metal), then say so. Your profile should resemble current reality. While it may be tempting to pose as your better-looking friend and enlist a consortium to write your blurb, this will only set you back in the dating game. Likewise, beware of the huge number of frauds who crawl the web.

Initial approaches should be brief and jaunty. Remember to spell out any sarcasm and avoid innuendos unless really asking for it. Officially it's rude not to respond to overtures, but don't be too charitable; all stalkers and weirdos should be reported and blocked. Once you've had it with someone, it's only polite to break it to them. If you end up being ignored, you should accept the fact graciously (and silently) once two messages are left unanswered. Don't delete your profile if you do get a date, or hassle your date to remove his, until two-way monogamy is established.

Speed dating can be classed as the conveyor belt approach to romance, so it's imperative to look as delectable as possible. Come armed with plenty of quirky questions and hold back from the boring, the personal and the heavy. Don't forget to flirt with those you like and take advantage of second chances during the breaks. If someone asks for your phone number be *en garde* – the system is in place to protect you from having to give out your details. When the scores roll in, don't gloat to your friend if the guy that she liked preferred you. Remember that men often conceal their cowardliness with coolness, so expect to make the first move.

Internet and speed dating may be new frontiers but many age-old dating rules still apply. Be kind to all of those who don't make the grade, and never entirely give yourself over to those that do. When it comes to internet dating, if you want to turn the artificial into real, then the sooner it migrates from the electronic ether into reality, the better. Over-optimism and anticipation must not be allowed to get out of hand, so once you are comfortable on email, someone needs to suggest meeting up. Indulge in a little internet-snooping beforehand, but remember that being suspiciously well-informed is creepy. Be generous with first impressions, as the forced situation often strips people of charm and ease. Running away if you don't like the look of them will bring terrible bad luck upon you.

Staying the Night

The first time you stay over will always be a potentially historic night. Sex is *numero uno* on the agenda, pressure to perform is high and afterwards, of course, everyone will pry – in fact, it has some similarities to a wedding night. The timing of the evening is critical, as maintaining male interest is a delicate balancing act. Make it too soon and risk looking easy, too slow and he may read it as a brush-off. The third date has become the accepted benchmark, but the right time is only really once you feel up for it.

Abstain from issuing or accepting invitations 'back to mine' if not carnally poised. Beware of boys' traps. Many will push for an early pay-off and then run away. First date frolics, even if blind in the fog of lust, are unwise. The exact timing must be judged on a case-by-

case basis, but remember, the most powerful tool is anticipation. Use it to your advantage.

Tonight is not the time to train him to tolerate your *laissez-faire* approach to grooming, so spend time preparing. Make sure you look well turned out, apply some scent to your pulse points. Underwear should always be petite and stylish. If staying at his, pack a bag (to include toothbrush, clean underwear and condoms). If hosting, do a bit of set-dressing (clean sheets, a plentiful wine supply, removal of ex-evidence). Lighting is critical. The easiest and least contrived option in the bedroom is the glow of street lighting, or candles for the really enamoured. Preparations should look unprepared – scattered rose petals should be saved for the wedding night.

Performance anxiety can be an anti-aphrodisiac, and alcohol's an unreliable crutch. If you begin to feel fried by the encounter, remember to have fun. Turn on the flirt mechanism, or discuss. It's good to talk, but stop before tears and dark confessions. Consummating the crush isn't necessarily a total foregone conclusion. If abstaining, however, be sure to protect his pride. Your change of heart can be taken personally; don't dish out blame, do apologise gently. If you misjudged your compatibility, it's kindest not to kick him out or walk out (cf. pride). An insuperable fatigue will draw a veil over most such matters.

If thus far unruffled, the love-in now beckons. Always keep up the humour quotient. This is a useful veneer for the naked reality of two people getting their rocks off for the first time and a

good moderator if things get clumsy (many relationships earn their Bad Sex Prize at this juncture). Communication is paramount. Speaking your mind (on contraception, preferences, feelings) is Route 1 to the sanctuary of familiarity, but a measured delivery is imperative here. Bedroom sports are safest played straight at first. Equilibrium should be found before going off-piste, though a mere twinkle in the eye can invite the bypass. Playing the lusty love-slave is never advisable, however. Consider the possibility that a flatmate could be in earshot. There is nothing quite as embarrassing as an audience (for most people, anyway).

The next morning will see you both in the sober, unforgiving light of day. You will need to confront the reality of smeared make-up, the squeamishness of daytime nakedness and mystique all but eroded. As tempting as it may be, running away won't do you any favours. The need to escape before sunrise should have been outgrown during adolescence. It is an important part of the dating process to brave out your first morning-after together. Make it a little easier by doing whatever makes you feel comfortable. Have a shower and put on make-up; if enslaved to self-consciousness, it's your prerogative to remove any possible concerns.

Determine to enjoy the morning. Relax over breakfast and the papers. If you are the host, toast and tea should be provided at the bare minimum. Be wary of creating too much fuss. Laying on the works is quite the giveaway gesture. Stay together for the day if so inclined, or give yourself some space by manufacturing a prior engagement. Conversation should not be forced. Enjoy a comfortable silence if it feels more appropriate. If you stayed at his, consider borrowing a top. Not only are you likely to look more cute in this than in a poor, tired version of yesterday's outfit, it's also a symbolic step into his world and an instant trophy.

Don't make assumptions, however. It's sweet to ask before you take his clothes or begin cooking breakfast; behaving like you've already moved in will have his commitment alarm bells screaming. Take a step back and stop him from getting too comfortable. Be good company, never clingy. Pick the optimum moment to make your exit. After a successful evening, try not to overstay your welcome – he should be falling over himself for you.

Playing the Plus-One

The Set-up

'Darling, let's go away for a few nights.' How divine. But what if the reality is an invitation to be your new man's plus-one on a business trip? It may sound about as romantic as a date in a service station, but half-empty thinking won't improve matters. The winning strategy is to play the gracious girlfriend. At worst, there will be endless hours on your own, or being ring-fenced with all the other plus-ones. At best, this is a chance to explore a new city and to bond (at someone else's expense). As with any first night away, challenges lie ahead – what will he make of your grooming habits? What if you become dumbstruck? – but this is also a test of self-sufficiency and adaptability. Treat it like a game. After all, you're not here to boost profits. You are here for him (and you), so claim your territory.

Arrival

Make like a scout and come prepared. Know your itinerary. Is it room service in a negligee for all meals, or will you be expected to be the *charmeuse* with the chief exec? It's horribly organised but do pack outfits rather than a random assortment of favourite pieces. Most men would be turned off by a vanity case the size of a house, so edit, edit, edit. If that only reduces it to the size of a bungalow, then stash any spillover products in your suitcase. On arrival, if he's offered to pick you up from the airport, run through your final checks (grooming, oral hygiene). Present him with a big kiss and a bottle of duty-free champagne. If you arrive but find that he is power-broking all day, then use this time to dress the suite. Making the room feel like yours should help to ease your awkwardness.

When Alone

Resist the mindset that says this is a duff trip; every destination will have some pleasures. Once you have located these, it's time to make him miss you. After all, you're likely to be having more fun than he is. Send flirty texts such as 'why don't you sneak out? The – insert cultural phenomenon here – is really stunning.' Use the time to refresh and pamper yourself (the hotel spa is there for a reason) or to plan a night out. Don't leave it up to him to organise the evening's events. He will have been working all day, and this way you get to do whatever you want. If after 24 hours you discover that you don't really get along (or it turns out that he has the personality of a rabid dog) then line up some passive entertainment – theatre followed by a jazz club followed by an 'oh my, is that the time?'.

Work or Play?

Rather like meeting the parents, mixing with his work colleagues is the time to perform, not pout. Know your place. This is his turf, you're his guest, he has more to lose than you. The cold reality is that your presence is his PR. Know your audience. If filthy jokes would be inappropriate, respect that. Flirting with his colleagues is permissible, possibly even encouraged. It bolsters the ego of the alpha male to think that his girl is desired by others, but be sure to play the *coquette* and not the *femme fatale*. If he has an early start the next day, you may want to make him a little bit late. The thrill of rule-breaking will be to your credit and he'll get nudge-nudge credibility from his colleagues. Another bonus: the drama of the misdemeanour might, just might, make him think about you in your absence.

Departure

Spending this much time together early on in a relationship can be revelatory. If your date turns out to have a roving eye and a wandering hand, then at least being in such close quarters has made you aware of the fact. If you don't want to see him again, be direct but kind. Explain to him 'sorry, but this is just not going to work out' (a reason for this perceived incompatibility is also owed). Don't forget to thank him for the trip. If, on the other hand, mutual approval abounds, the goodbye should come naturally enough. Simply thank, hug, kiss, without going overboard. Quite possibly you'll now feel indebted to him but, apart from sincere gratitude towards both him and his boss, you don't owe him anything if it was his idea, his invitation and on company expenses. The score is even.

His Friends

Meeting his friends can have all the appeal of being thrown to the lions. But remember, while they may all be vetting you, it's also a chance for you to scope out the new boyfriend through the kind of company he keeps. You should also be a little flattered. Boys are notoriously guarded with their gang, so letting you in suggests that you're up to it.

Surviving the all-male lion's den requires a sublimation of all girly waffle and sentiment. Masculine small talk is a battle of wits and ego. Expect to fight to be heard, only to be heckled off. If volleying one-liners is too ambitious, aim for a circumspect middle ground. In truth, it's important to be yourself. A little concerted effort to get involved is always appreciated, and a ready smile rarely fails to charm. Early on, it might be safer to stay in the shadows than be ripped to shreds in a rush to break the group. Ease yourself in with smaller, girl-friendly events (give big sporting occasions a wide berth) or stick to the fringes for one-on-ones with more sensitive types. You can disarm most boys with a compliment – a rarity amongst the brethren.

While your girlfriends may be dying to meet your boyfriend, his friends are unlikely to care much about you. Don't take this as an insult. Men are straight shooters in conversation. Their humour is bound in mockery so, again, don't take offence where none is due. Be careful not to over-think a situation (a particularly female weakness), but come

armed with your senses of survival and humour. Indulging in soppy affection – especially in front of his single best mate – will result in instant relegation and public ribbing for both you and your man, as will any displays of wing clipping (e.g. lambasting him, dragging him home). Territorial urges towards his female friends must be quickly quelled. Despite your suspicions, it's unlikely that he's had them all. They wield much power, so try to get them onside.

Don't shirk away from round-buying duties but don't overdo it. Matching the boys' intake and getting ruinously drunk is unlikely to afford you instant inclusion. While you or he can criticise your own respective friends, you can't criticise each other's. This will only be taken as a personal snub, and you will feel uncomfortable the next time you see them. You may also be wrong, as warming to his friends is like listening to a new album. It may need several chances before it takes.

Bide your time before introducing him to your friends. Make sure you're confident that the relationship has legs first; cracks will be all the more gaping in front of a third party. The scenario must be carefully managed. Drinks are less pressured than dinner and mixed groups less intimidating than all-girl gatherings. Ease him in with friends that he might get on with. Some men can be taken anywhere while others are pure petulance when forced into being on show – nurture him.

The Mini-Break

Be Prepared

Before you buy a car, you take it for a test drive. Similarly, the mini-break is a jaunty little foray into being up close and personal without having to stay there. You might have notched up several nights together – you may even have a drawer at his – but there are plenty more discoveries around the corner so make sure you are fully prepared. To look good at all times (equipped only with a weekend bag) do some location research and weather checks. Implement an underwear and grooming overhaul. Feeling at ease in your own skin might not come naturally to all, but it can be assisted. Those who are conversationally challenged might like to bring facilitators such as travel games, cards or local guidebooks. For those whose sociability is likely to expire, pack some reading material.

Destination

Such is the (charming) hold of tradition in dating that men are likely to want to take control here. He may decide to surprise you so prepare to be grateful. If you are expecting Monaco and get Margate, express only excitement and enthusiasm. He will have chosen the destination carefully with you in mind – worry more about that. If you choose the location together, bear in mind what you want from the break. Cities are good for new relationships which require stimulants. If you are at all nervous about having enough to talk about, choose somewhere with plenty of culture and nightlife to give you lots of distractions to discuss. If the aim of the trip is to get away from routine and other people, then the countryside bestows space. The focus is entirely on the two of you.

Money

Along with logistics, money can be a niggling obstruction to freewheeling romance. While it is deeply unsexy to ask, this is a discussion that needs to be had, as it's important to know what the other can afford. If it turns out you are unequally matched financially and he is generous enough to insist on subsidising you (yet another vestige of inequality to be occasionally indulged), it's polite to chip in with a round of drinks here, a pub lunch there. If funds are limitless on both sides, you can eschew this discussion altogether but should both try to take turns in paying. All of this sounds rather unromantic – romance and money are like oil and water – but money can dictate how you spend your trip. You both need to take turns in the driving seat. Concede to his choices, as he should to yours.

Successful Navigation

Relax. There may be many points of interest on your cultural clipboard, but their purpose is only to buoy your experience. Take things seriously easy. Pay heed to the dynamic of undivided attentions. These are an important accelerator of relationships, but the cumulative effects can be rather trying. Remember to give each other a little privacy. For some, however, becoming thoroughly fed up of togetherness is just a matter of time. If this is the case, try to remain diplomatic and deal with it privately. Find yourself some space or indulge in literary escapism. Remember that silence can be more positive than fractious conversation. Be sure to close the weekend on a high (even if it takes a concerted effort). Enjoy celebratory champagne at the airport, laughter and lightness on the way home.

Meeting the Parents

It's quite a gesture on his part and one that might suggest some commitment. Not only that, but here's an opportunity to gauge your boyfriend's prospective hairline count by seeing his father's. Of course, you'll be assessed for suitability to continue the family bloodline. Just display some proto-mothering skills in the kitchen and the rest only calls for a good balance between being yourself and best behaviour.

Sniff out background information in advance. Are they strict or relaxed? Will it be lunch for 20 on the verandah and dinner in tails, or TV dinners and hourly altercations? Any no-go conversational topics (e.g. neighbours from hell, black sheep) and any specialist subjects?

Rather boringly, it's best to dress on the conservative side. Present yourself as a fine, upstanding young lady, and lure them in with elegant presentation. Overdressing is unrelaxing for you and intimidating to them, while any scruffy or ripped clothes will prompt youth-of-today accusations. Packing both smart and casual outfits should cover you for all eventualities.

It's handshakes and Mr/Mrs to you until invited otherwise. Remember their rulebook is older than yours. Failing to take a present is an oversight by their book and a wasted chance for brownie points. Nothing too adventurous, so a plant and a decent bottle of wine will suffice; be more original if you dare.

You may detect hostility from the mother for threatening to take away her boy, but ignore awkward passive aggression and be the pro-houseguest. Step up interpersonal skills and table manners, and affect total disinterest in your mobile. Mucking in is imperative and serves as a good icebreaker. Take the initiative with basic chores, so don't offer to wash up, just do it. Never try to compete with the mother – let her rule her domestic roost.

Resist all inclinations to lean on your boyfriend, but follow his lead. Observe how relaxed he is and then step up the formality slightly. What might be normal for him (e.g. swearing, eating from the fridge) isn't for you. Getting more drunk than the parents could raise an eyebrow or two, while angry hangovers are never the mark of a girl good enough for their boy. That said, a little sherry tipsiness all round can be a bonding moment, but beware of the situational overdose and refrain from any entwinement with your boyfriend; keep that rulebook forever in your sights.

Well-informed conversation with a bite of opinion is the ticket. Modestly promote yourself; you have interesting friends, brilliant parents, a great career. Avoid controversy but, if someone else brings it up, gently embrace it. Debate with reason, but don't take parents to task. Never gang up on your boyfriend to get other family members on side and note that gushing compliments will ring out as creepy and insincere. Never whinge about the injustices of your life.

If you are sharing a bedroom with your boyfriend, be super-discreet. If in separate rooms, your boyfriend should do the bed-hopping. Only he can steal down unlit corridors and avoid creaking floorboards and alarm systems; only he should face the music if caught.

Afterwards, write a thank you letter within a week. When debriefing with your boyfriend, note double standards. He's allowed to criticise his parents, but you are not.

Hold your horses before taking him home to your parents. If you're uneasy about calling him 'your boyfriend', then it's too soon. He'll be scared off, while your parents will sense the strain and may wrongly disapprove of him.

Warn him of any family oddities or off-limits behaviour. Prime him on their pet hates and weak spots and ask your parents to leave all the ugly-duckling evidence in the closet.

Take the lead, but let him assert his own presence and personality. Don't tease him, embarrass him or dent his male pride. Offer some guidance and keep an eye out for pitfalls. Remember the spotlight is on him and, for most of us, that's not much fun.

On Holiday

The Romantic Getaway

Doubtless it'll be a voyage of discovery. The test is whether it involves cocktails, silvery seas and moonlit skinny-dipping or, less blissfully, intolerable bad habits and bad moods after two weeks in very close confines. Diverting any potential misunderstanding takes patience; we're all prone to some holiday tensions.

Choosing a holiday destination can be perversely strenuous, especially as men and women are totally different creatures. To escape an almighty power struggle, try to compromise. If a certain someone can't sit still for long, perhaps that sleepy beach holiday is one-sided. Likewise, don't surrender to an extreme adventure holiday if all you want to do is kick back. By meeting each other in the middle, you'll need to unleash your inner lad and extricate yourself from the comfort of your sun lounger.

Preparation

When you're planning a holiday *à deux*, responsibilities can be halved. Take the initiative and confirm flights, book taxis, sort insurance, check passports. He can take his turn later by ordering cocktails and tipping porters.

Don't leave grooming and packing to the last minute. Throw in the odd smart outfit – just in case he decides to wine and dine you – and your very best underwear. Mix'n'match that capsule wardrobe. Perfect hair and make-up will be blown out of the water when you're on holiday (perhaps it's best he knows what he is letting himself in for). If you can't face it, however, book in for a fake tan and some grooming treatments.

Mutual soul-searching is inevitably likely to raise some thorny truths (ex-loves, personal baggage). Don't let any new information cloud your holiday.

Getting Closer

Holidays are a real relationship odyssey. Various topics of discussion will present themselves, all in the name of getting to know each other. So, if you haven't already racked up your first argument, it is more than likely to land on holiday. It's imperative to rule out the Number One trigger of arguments: money. Pool resources or take turns in paying; don't ever quibble. Even with money out of the equation, moods brew and nerves may be tested (this is the cold reality of spending your waking hours together).

Be patient with bad habits and off-beat sleeping and eating patterns. It's unlikely that you'll want to sleep or eat the same, or even talk as much as each other. Few boys are mind-readers so if something bothers you, negotiate and (briefly) discuss, but don't forget about romance and cocktails at sunset.

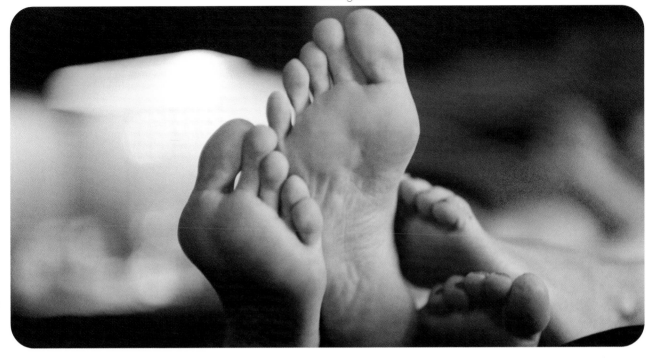

Couple Conduct

Under the giddy spell of love, nothing else seems to matter. Unfortunately, it does, and neglected friends can come to resent the boyfriend. Unless you are intending to elope to the end of the earth together, those around you need to be kept sweet. Also, leaving yourself without a potential shoulder to cry on is regrettably short-sighted.

In the throes of a new relationship, it's easy to lose friends and alienate people by becoming a half-person, i.e. giving up on your own life and leaning on his. When without him, never speak of you both as a single entity ('we think this') or appear entirely hijacked by him ('my boyfriend says that'). If invited out, don't refuse to commit until you have checked with your 'significant other' (or other term of dependency). It is polite to consult your amour, but to announce

it only makes friends begrudge his hold on you. Never boycott invitations that don't extend to a plus one.

Maintain the united front and avoid indulging in public bickering. Arguing with your man in public is a bad idea; the louder and longer it goes on, the more foolish you'll look. Cultivating a reputation for leaving scars on events attended together will always result in diminished invitations.

Restrain public displays of affection. Public cooing, whispering, stroking and pet-name calling will communicate the message that others are invisible and irrelevant, be they strangers or friends. If entertaining company, you will leave the poor lemon ruing their decision to meet up with you. N.B. holding hands and a quick peck are acceptable for most people.

Popular couples strike the balance. They don't take each other for granted – no matter how familiar things have become – and manage to preserve some independence. They join in with life, rather than cling to their comfort zone. They will sneak off for a snog and realise that a clandestine kiss is much more fun than catching friends' eyes rolling again. They keep in touch with their own friends and don't always turn up together. By holding on to a vestige of their independent lives, they have something to fall back on if/when the relationship sours.

Curiosity killed the cat. Don't probe your boyfriend for details about his ex, especially if you can't handle picturing them in each other's loving clutches. If you have to meet her, prepare yourself to weather a rough ride, but maintain

absolute grace and composure. Even if she is an evil bitch, he will probably still think quite fondly of her (this issue isn't worth labouring), and he won't savour your criticisms or be endeared to your irritating insecurities.

An unfortunate love triangle forms when his ex is a friend of yours. It's very dangerous territory; you are unlikely to receive forgiveness and quite likely to lose a friend. If felled by Cupid's arrow, however, with no choice but to submit (he had better be worth it), be sure that their relationship is over. You must have the dreaded conversation with her; it is only correct that she hears it from you (even if she already knows that you're together). Brace yourself for ostracism from mutual friends. Being couply in front of her (or your friends) will ruin any chances of acceptance. If you're in

for just a quick fling, be sure to keep it quiet. It may seem very devious, but is ultimately less harrowing for all.

Rules apply to your ex too. Talking about his muscles, meteoric career and eight-figure inheritance will emasculate your current beau. He must be totally confident that your ex is history.

Cohabitation isn't a life sentence, but familiarity can breed contempt. It's a sad fact that the longer you live with someone, the worse you are likely to treat them. It takes a concerted effort to resist this slippery slope and keep things wonderfully rosy.

Be considerate. It may feel slightly unnatural, but always say please and thank you, ask him before inviting your friends back and don't desert him for better invitations. Share the chores and cook together. Agree on a division of

labour, establish the ground rules and don't apportion blame if something goes wrong.

Create your own spaces and supply your own TVs to avoid remote control war. Respect privacy and never open each other's post. Be business-minded and reliable with money and bills. Don't buy before living together; a test run is an essential check on the stability (or fragility) of the relationship. Claim your territory if moving into his. Likewise, if he is moving into yours, give him joint ownership (physically, not literally). Give him the space you'd expect, not just a drawer and a toothbrush holder. Always keep a bottle of champagne to hand in the fridge and celebrate happy times. Never underestimate the wonders of an undisturbed housebound romantic evening in together.

Infidelity

The Rules

A relationship means a total reduction of choice, whereas singledom equals a maximisation of choice. Crimes of the heart stem from greed (not need) and infidelity isn't an open-and-shut case. It's a spectrum of degrees and, if you wouldn't want your other half carrying on as you are, then unfaithfulness may be a fitting charge – emotionally if not physically.

Occasionally an affair is a truer and longer-lasting love than expected but, for most, the short term buzz is eroded by longer-lasting guilt and heartbreak. So, before playing away, consider the risks and what is at stake. If you're still powerless to resist, ensure that the truth is tightly contained. Observers will pour scorn on your transgressions and gossip has wings – confessions should only ever come from you.

Adulterers

Adulterers live like spies. They need to be constantly on the alert, cleverly fabricating double lives, covering tracks and scuttling around on dark moonless nights. You can't be too cautious and need to avoid arousing the suspicions of your better half, friends, family and even work colleagues. No secret is ever totally watertight.

Destroy receipts you cannot easily explain your way out of, and be sure to delete any incriminating text messages (received or sent). Be very wary of using email, especially if your password isn't a state secret. Avoid telling elaborate lies (always more likely to be rumbled) and never use friends as alibis without their permission beforehand (always a big favour). Secrets and lies are always corrosive – you'll need to ask yourself regularly if it's all worth it.

Mistress

If you are playing the mistress, keep the secret on a definite need-to-know basis. Confidants are important, but choose one that has no connection whatsoever to the couple and, again, steel yourself for their disapproval. Remember that a married man usually wants a fling with no strings. He rarely leaves his wife and, if he did, he may well do the same to you. This is a choice best suited to women with commitment issues.

Plan B (the affair) is not necessarily the better option; it is an indication that Plan A (the relationship) needs fixing. Don't be cowardly about confronting this as, after all, running two concurrent plans is far more problematic than one (broken or otherwise). You've heard it before, but don't be reckless with other people's hearts and don't put up with people who are reckless with yours.

In Flagrante

Parents

Parental respect should always overrule the thrill of danger. Cross-generational caught-in-the-act situations won't be quickly forgotten by either party. At his parents' house, it is his responsibility to apologise first and smooth things over for you. Fleeing prematurely will only suggest cowardice. With your parents, it's up to you to bite the bullet first, but make sure he apologises too.

The case where all parties are fully aware of the deed but all stay shtum is a conundrum. Do you apologise or just sweep it under the carpet? It depends on the parents, so with sterner parents the less said the better. N.B. biological make-up means that boys will readily lose sight of the inappropriateness of sex under parents' roofs. It is therefore up to the girl to be strict in completely risky instances.

Flatmates

For many, it's an eventuality that one day you'll be caught by your flatmates. Various scenarios can ensue and blame can be apportioned but, ultimately, the sooner you can see the funny side, the better home life will be.

Flatmates will inevitably barge into your bedroom unannounced. The event may embarrass them more than you as you can't see what they can. They must apologise as soon as is appropriate.

If you are caught having a quickie on the sofa (or worse still, on their bed), they have every right to be furious with you – it's a totally grim violation. You must apologise immediately and then compensate with a fitting and generous gift. Remember, what they don't know will never hurt them, so save adventures beyond your own bedroom for when home alone.

Saying Goodbye

The act of splitting up with someone must be direct, decisive and, above all, kind. Dumpees deserve some mercy in such humbling times; feelings should be protected. Fictitious excuses won't make the problem go away, however, and any ambiguity looks dangerously like an open window to the desperate. The coward who delays the eventuality only gives false hope. Of course, when discarding total love-rats, a ceremonial dumping is quite acceptable: 'it's not me, it's you'.

Disposing of short-lived liaisons is straightforward. If there are insufficient sparks to keep the pilot light aflame, it's fine to extinguish the fling by email or telephone, but texting is one notch too heartless. Quietly ducking out of particularly undeveloped affairs can be preferable to the potential arrogance of stating that it's over. Heartbreakers are best advised not to entertain their casualties in extended texting or email exchange post-split – this will only feed their anger or hopes.

More deeply rooted relationships deserve a more elaborate burial. The time has to be right and sufficient time must be dedicated. Face to face is the only acceptable medium. As the black clouds gather, consider your reasoning and start issuing some warning signs. The long-term lover deserves a (gentle) explanation. If it's genuinely nothing to do with them, let them know or risk leaving them scarred with insecurities. Sometimes, being nice isn't the natural inclination at this stage and bitterness or blame might feel more appropriate. Unless in the midst of 'irreconcilable differences', it's more sensible to keep it amicable. This isn't always the easiest way – things may well get worse before they get better.

If you are dumped, accept the fact that he's just not that into you. Climb out of the wreckage and set to work on reducing your dependence on him. Heartbreak hotel is a lonely, indulgent place, so distract yourself by trying to re-engage with old friends and new prospects (comforting even if rebounds are rarely real). It is quite possible that he's mixing his messages and, if this is the case, heed his behaviour over his words. Find out if ending it is really just a temporary decision and then move on accordingly. If he is that into you, he'll do the chasing.

The aftermath can bring emotional free fall, so keep your dignity. Rein in rash compulsions: no pitiful pleadings for reinstatement; no extractions of promises for future reconciliations; no emotional blackmail. Who wants to be with a guy who was browbeaten into it? If prone to drunken dialling, delete his number from your phone or, better still, avoid excesses while you are grieving. Midnight sobbings will show you up as a wreck. You may want to compose a letter or email – it may offer some kind of closure – but sit on it for a few days before sending it, and don't send it at all if there is any inkling of doubt.

The ritual of disentanglement varies according to whether you hope to be friends or whether you never want to set eyes on him ever again. It's normal to feel muddled. Rushing into friend status is confusing; a separation period helps the healing process. Ex-sex only tightens the knot of emotions. At least one party (usually the girl) will still have feelings and being the moth to an old flame is dangerous. Time often masks original pain and sex can just reveal it all over again.

Profiteering from any break-up (i.e. keeping CDs, books etc.) has terrible karmic implications; a redistribution of possessions back to him will afford an altruistic glow (returning gifts won't be appreciated). Possessions, haunts and friends you have accumulated must be offered to the wounded party; exes that are friends might be less divisive about such things.

Once you are happily rehabilitated, it's sensible to quietly inform exes who move in the same circles as you of new liaisons. If you're not on close enough terms, hand the information over to the rumour mill and let people get to work. Serial monogamists who already have their next victim lined up should hold off from broadcast until it's a sure thing, and delay going public for a while to avoid any accusations of crossover. An ex's close friends/family should only be pursued if you are experiencing earth-shaking sensations that they could truly be The One.

The Ex

Exes are like black holes. The danger of proximity is explicit, but somehow the gravitational pull is irresistible. It really wouldn't do to still be hiding from him in supermarkets at the age of 65, so try to deal with it now.

If preparation is possible, some like to restore pride with a revenge dress (nothing too obvious, just insouciantly sexy). Without any advance knowledge, seeing him may come as a shock. You have to say hello (politely). Try to think kind thoughts about him; it might take some faking, but better behaviour from you encourages him to behave better back (win-win). Ask him how he is. If he asks after you, be strong, even if you're still licking your wounds. Avoid being flippant and don't flirt with other men in front of him. Stay in control. Divert any emotional downpours onto a good

friend, in a private place. Even if you did the dirty on him, a rapprochement is the grown-up path. If experiencing severe cringe-out, minimise meetings to avoid being a bitch. New boyfriends and girlfriends will eventually enter the equation, but keep the initial meeting brief. Don't flatter or flirt with your ex in front of your new squeeze.

Conversely, if you wish to be friends with your ex, you will also need to be friends with his new girlfriend. This will take time and requires a suppression of small-mindedness (on both sides). She will need implicit reassurance that you are over him; you must deal with their physical affections. It is too idealistic for many but, at the very least, it prevents all that annoyance of not being able to go out because 'she' might be there. Inevitably, you'll have a lot in common.

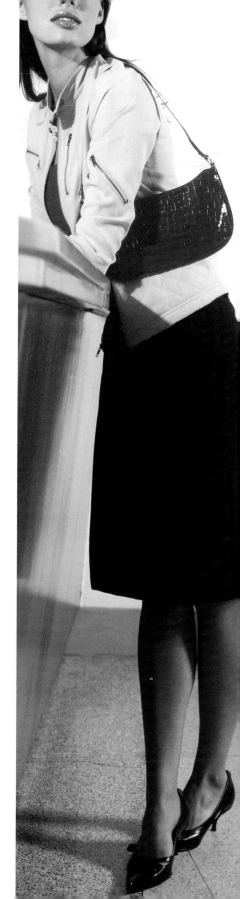

No-Shows

Finding yourself all out of date is one of the most humiliating non-events for single girls. It's impossible not to take it personally and is also a reminder never to be as selfish yourself.

It's civil to allow about half an hour's grace before putting in a call. Try to be without prejudice as maybe something dreadful has happened, or maybe he's just round the corner. If he doesn't pick up the phone, you are hereby entitled to cut your losses. Leave a brief polite message – benefit of the doubt is still the best approach here – but, from this time on, keep a dignified silence with the deserter. It's very much his duty to make amends and, if he doesn't, you can move on. Remember you have an audience of waiters, bar staff and other neighbouring customers, so what's left of your dignity must be well preserved

by keeping your cool. Likewise, if he cries off at the final hour, try to hold it together (you don't need him, right?). Always get straight back on the phone to more reliable friends and turn your evening around – wallowing in self-pity is for total losers.

Standing up a date is superlatively bad form. If you're the one doing the jilting, bear a few things in mind. If it's down to losing your nerve, remember it might be now or never as your date is unlikely to present himself for potential mortification again. If it's down to a real change of heart, remember that it will be an interesting evening whatever the outcome, and it needn't end in liplock. If insistent that it is not to be, or if there are practical impediments to the date, do the honourable thing and call him as soon as you can.

Understanding Men

Gender Difference

Some sweeping gender characteristics: girls worry, boys are laid back; girls are manipulative, boys like things straight-up; girls plan, boys live in the moment; girls like to make homes, boys like to drink beer and watch sport on TV; girls love shopping, boys hate it; girls nag, boys need nagging.

Surgically conjoined relationships tend to implode. Give him some space and he will get a perspective on quite what a catch you are. He'll then start to miss you and give you all the attention you crave (and deserve). Do not resent the time he spends with his friends and realise that time apart is healthy.

Acknowledging and accepting the entrenched polarity between the sexes is an important step in understanding men; meeting them in the middle an optional second.

Communication

While women over-process issues from every conceivable perspective, men are much less likely to devote any thought space to you and your feelings. Unless you communicate your emotions and expectations, he is unlikely to be aware of them. Always collect your thoughts before you talk.

Boys tend to forget birthdays and anniversaries – just accept this and help him be less rubbish. Dropping hints will be more effective than sulky guilt trips.

Men can't multitask. If they are in the pub drinking beer, do not expect them to call you as well. Think of it as oversight rather than offence. Also, for many men, email and telephones are merely organisational tools. Boys will send brief text messages, not lengthy essays. Technology isn't a substitute for face to face communication.

Jealousy

Understand the male condition. He is biologically programmed to zone in on female assets (as indeed are women to men's; they're just more subtle and less interested). Let him flirt; you'll seem all the more attractive and secure for not reacting to it. Don't be tempted to ask if he's attracted to that belle in a skimpy bikini – of course he is. It will upset you and only annoy him, so such questions are best left unasked. Don't test his self-confidence by marvelling at other men as the male green-eyed monster is very ferocious, so admire quietly.

Some men constantly battle against their evolutionary urges. Preventing any infidelity is, in part, about making the effort and not becoming the lazy lover. If he starts talking about loyalty over fidelity, however, dispose of him before he strays too far.

Nagging

Women nag because men can't defer gratification (now: TV, food, beer; later: chores). They are less exacting about domestic standards and reminders may be necessary, but choose your moment wisely and stay unruffled. Whining will only reduce your impact. Playing the henpecking harridan won't get the job done faster – it will just make you less lovable. Rather than nag, tell him what the problem is and lure him into action with a softly-softly strategy. Encourage him to think it was all his idea and not your heavy hand.

Unlike women, men don't do detail. He won't be interested in an exhaustive account of how X fell out with Y, or how Z then came along and saved the day. Don't bang on; save the trivia for your girlfriends, and don't take umbrage at his indifference.

Commitment

Emotional availability only comes on his terms. Needling him into a proposal or cohabitation may provoke a sense of entrapment, and caged animals crave escape. Looking needy has little allure, so be cool and he may come to these decisions alone. Proceed with caution, however, and don't wait a lifetime for the commitment-phobe.

A premature declaration of love is likely to make him bolt right back to the boys. Never ever utter it unless you are entirely positive (and not at the bottom of your tenth Martini).

A man's sex organ is in his trousers and a woman's is in her head, so never sleep with a friend. Men can be more dissociative about the deed (your brain is likely to complicate matters). Things may never be the same again. Largely inadvisable.

Proposals

So, off you go on that trip to Tuscany; cue an invitation to the coveted 'Mrs' upgrade. Conceal any disappointment, however, if the ring fails to materialise. Such a tiny question is terrifying for him and many bail out first time round. Even if you're presented with every clue short of a bent knee, file the thought away or else risk casting a dark shadow over a perfectly good holiday.

Marriage is bound up in all manner of traditional rituals. Formalities begin with him asking his future in-laws, so if your parents start acting funny, count it as a big clue. Inevitably, some prefer to bypass this and ask the girl first. If the proposal comes before permission, the parents must be asked/told (depending on your take) soon afterwards. They can't actually say no, so permission is largely ceremonial.

If his taste in rings is a bit off, don't let it dampen the thrill. See if it grows on you – but not enough for all friends and family to see it – and, if it doesn't, gently let him know. Don't endure a ghastly ring for a (married) lifetime out of shyness or kindness. According to the rules, the man is to expected pay once or twice his net monthly salary on a sparkler. It's nice, but not obligatory, to return the gesture with a lovely gift such as a watch. More modern couples split the cost of the ring.

There is much talk about the four 'Cs' of a diamond: cut, colour, clarity and carat. Most people are only really impressed by carat, carat, carat and carat (i.e. size). Platinum is currently the most popular metal for the mount, but it won't always be that way. The very anxious ring-buyer might also seek the counsel of his loved one's good friends to help find a ring to suit. Clearly, the fewer people who know beforehand, the more chance of romantic surprise.

Engagement will bring an awful lot of attention. People will make instant judgements about you and your fiancé, your lifestyle and how much he adores you, largely through the ring on your finger. Your ring will virtually become public property (so make sure your nails are manicure perfect). However, it's too silly to start married life in debt just to impress others with a lump of carbon, especially if there are homes, weddings and honeymoons to save for.

Turning down the man who desires your hand is always a secret honour; broadcasting such news brings shame and resentment. To lessen his private humiliation, never ever laugh, however preposterous the idea. Avoid blurting out excuses and stay calm. If you are in no doubt that you must say no, refuse in a delicate manner and be gracious. Respect his feelings and his ego; this is quite some overture and should be respected thus. If you are unsure, ask for more time. Bailing out later on will cause a considerably greater loss of face for both parties. If he's gone the whole hog and got a ring, return it to him (likewise, if you decide to call off an engagement) and don't wait for him to ask for it. If he is absolutely insistent that you keep it (bear in mind the knock to his pride when asking for a refund), or if he jumps ship, then you could (quietly) flog it. What else is a girl to do? After all, you can rest assured that no future husband will appreciate a collection of diamond skeletons.

Rules of Engagement

Announcements

Parents come first, then family, friends and colleagues. Your inner circle should be honoured with a telephone call, but peripheral friends should settle for an email bulletin. The announcement may feel desperately self-important to more reserved couples, but friends don't like to hear by word of mouth.

There is the traditional medium of the Forthcoming Marriages column of the newspaper, but it's just another job for the bride's parents to organise and, unless all friends and family are slaves to social news, it shouldn't be the only means of announcement. If so desired, wording should read: 'Mr P La-di-Dah and Miss V Blah-Blah/The engagement is announced between Peter, second son of Mr and Mrs Simon La-di-Dah of Lewes, East Sussex, and Victoria, only daughter of Mr and Mrs John Blah-Blah of Chipping Campden, Gloucestershire'. The groom-to-be's mother should write to the bride-to-be's parents expressing her happiness at the engagement, but to insist on it would be old-fashioned.

Far more practical is to introduce both sets of parents. Owing to the high incidence of family dysfunction, this is often a stressful encounter. Conspire in advance and decide who will pick up the bill. Traditionally this is down to the bride's side but, in modern times, the handsomely salaried groom may like to lay claim to alpha male status here. Be well armed with good small talk as the meeting may well require considerable buoyancy aids.

Congratulations

For better or for worse, life will change after The Question. There is gratuitous romance, weeks of champagne and (possibly less enjoyable) free entry into a new family. Friends and relatives will want to fete you. Prepare to sign away your privacy and get ready to present an endlessly polite public persona and unity for the duration.

Letters of congratulations are due once the engagement is made public; the form is charmingly head-in-sand. They should be addressed to him or her but never jointly – heaven forbid the act of living in sin is recognised – so write to the side you were friends with first or are related to. Modern day well-wishers don't see why the couple can't be congratulated together, be it with champagne, flowers, cards, emails or texts. Close friends must send cards and above.

Two officially become one when it comes to invitations. Never invite one half of the engaged couple without the other, but cleaved couples must accept any separation and never insist that the other is invited. After all, it's a chance to flirt unsupervised once again.

Length of engagement varies and is dependent on the scale of the event to be organised and the time of year in which you wish to tie the knot. Six to twelve months is average as it's hard to organise a traditional wedding in much less. A shotgun wedding, however, can be set up in days, and a commitment-phobe can delay the big day for years.

Parties and Cancellations

There's no obligation, but it's an excuse to throw a party and good groundwork for pre-wedding day mixing of friends. Tradition expects parents to host and pay for an engagement party. It can be co-hosted by both sets but, predictably, this can create complications. There is, as usual, an expectation on the bride's family and, if your parents do decide to take the honour, then it is customary for your father to make an informal speech and raise a toast. You could, of course, throw the party yourselves. While guests aren't really expected to bring presents, something small from good friends and relatives is a nice gesture. A card never hurt anybody, especially if neglected on announcement of the news.

If you suddenly want out, or realise that your true destiny lies in others' arms, then the engagement should be broken off. Gossip will earn its keep, so tell some key voices and the news will broadcast quickly. If an announcement is necessary, the wording should read: 'The marriage arranged between Mr Peter La-di-Dah and Miss Victoria Blah-Blah will not take place'.

If the wedding invitations have been sent out, then a note/card must also be sent to all of the guests announcing the cancellation. The reason for calling it off does not need to be disclosed, and any engagement or premature wedding presents should be returned. It may be painful and embarrassing, but view it as favourable to a showdown at the altar with a real live audience.

At Home

Perfect Hostess

To be perfect at any skill is annoying for others to be around; to be too perfect a hostess can be counterproductive. To avoid control freakishness, the key is to focus on social – rather than material – perfection. The tangible devices of any event (food, drink, music) are nothing without what is the main constituent of atmosphere: people. While guests are unpredictable and largely beyond the control of even the most accomplished hostess, the socially gifted regard them as active ingredients to be cooked up to form the core of a rollicking party – a sticky, fruity, social jam.

When picking the guest list, include a healthy risk factor; new friends should be mixed with old, familiar friends with strangers and opposites with alikes. Your invitations will set the tone for the entire event, so think printed cards for formal affairs, emails for casual ones and impromptu phone calls for right-nows. Replies may roll in but be sure to cater for any no-shows, nos-that-mean-yesses and the plain uninvited; you should always over-cater. Be ready to accommodate all with the-more-the-merrier spirit. Give a clear dress code briefing (and make it a fun one). The hostess will be personally responsible for elevating the party aesthetic with a suitably gorgeous outfit.

On the day, factor in extra boudoir time to allow for a last-minute dash. Leave some time to put the finishing touches to any ingestible delights you have planned; these should be creative without being overly ambitious or in any way showy. Missing your deadline (the doorbell) will sow stress upon all. On entering, guests should be swiftly grafted into the action, and a suitable drink pressed into their hands. Guests' offerings should all be received with equally glowing gratitude. The hostess is under no obligation to open guests' inferior wines or chocolates, but should be quick to take the hint if guests have been kind enough to bring chilled champagne. Be on hand to infect your guests with cheer and ease (even if a little faking is required), so, if needs be, farm out any banal kitchen duties to friends. The hostess must circulate to check that guests are fed and watered and ensure that the social jam is stirred. Introduce those that might get on and corral the social lepers, but do all this without being overbearing, looking like you're working the room, or actually just working. Overfill glasses at your peril; any ensuing disasters may be your fault.

Playing the put-upon hostess is such a mood killer, so avoid any little dramas. Trotting around after guests with stain removers and sponges won't do your credibility any favours. Relax about such materialistic concerns and only clear up as much as is necessary; control freaks and wild parties remain mutually exclusive. If guests care to do drugs, turning a blind eye rather than taking issue should ensure a smoother ride (unless this puts them in serious danger). Being in the safety net of your own crash pad is no excuse to get utterly wrecked.

At going-home time, some type of performance is usually required to clear the decks of any stragglers (you should probably worry if not – the touchstone of any good party is always contentedly settled guests). Begin to increase the pressure incrementally with yawns, talk of early-morning meetings and offers to call cabs. The veteran hostess always has taxi numbers to hand. Some hosts volunteer to give their stamp collection an airing. Others just go to bed.

Disasters you will face will rarely be anything other than alcohol-induced. A perfect hostess will grit her teeth and adopt an 'oh-well-these-things-happen' equanimity and then get over it (very quickly). If any vomiting occurs, it's your responsibility to tidy up, but delegation is permitted. The spare room/sofa must be willingly donated to unconscious guests. Deal with all breakages and any spillages *sans* drama. Kind offers of compensation should be refused, with exceptions made for family heirlooms and serious kit. Laugh off all verbal *contretemps* as party politics but, in the case of full-on fisticuffs, the boys may need to be enlisted to get things under control. Think carefully before involving them, however, as situations may spiral. Calling cabs is an option (though just slightly imperious). Indecent proposals are, in theory, only an asset to a party's reputation, but they can be distressing. Deftly separate the offender and the offended or, in the worst-case scenario, evict the over-amorous.

As underpreparing is a recipe for disaster, the perfect hostess must be prepared for Those Who Pop In. This is a dying custom that sadly must, at least outwardly, be encouraged. Impromptu visits are fortunately best enjoyed in a relaxed fashion. The needs of all but the most demanding guest should be served by a bar, a well-stocked larder and an enthusiastic sense of hospitality.

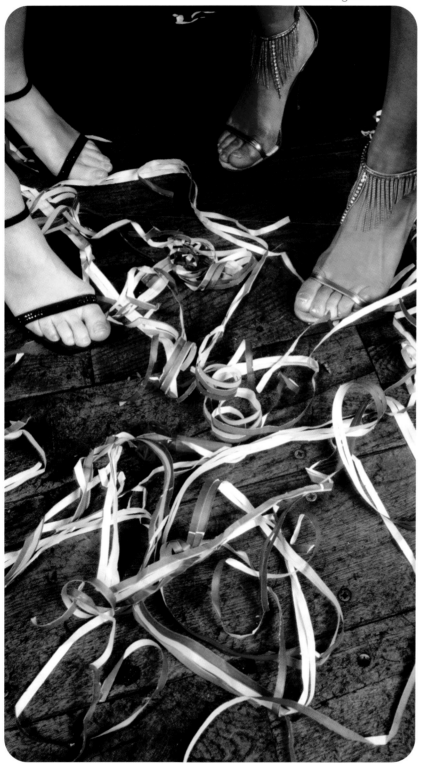

Drinks Party

Getting Going

Parties are brilliantly self-serving. The hostess cherry-picks the company, the food and drink, and the evening's soundtrack and surroundings, all to suit her tastes. They even enable a little social engineering – throwing a *soirée* is a cunning strategy to bring a potential love interest near, and to do so without having to confess to any such desires. Parties are always a bit wobbly to start off with and can require considerable nurturing before the stabilisers can be removed. Being the hostess requires radar-like sensitivity; be on hand to mingle with newcomers, keep antennae twitching for strays on the fringe and look out for casualties in the making. Once things become more atomic, a kind of circular energy will take over and you can safely relax (until, that is, the stretchers need to be wheeled out).

The Bar

A party without alcohol is like a car without petrol; it can be pushed along for a bit but will eventually grind to a halt. Running dry is quite disastrous for a party's engine. While providing a fully stocked bar is above and beyond the call of duty, accommodating all tastes (wine, beer, cocktails, softies) is basic party democracy. Even BYO calls for a good alcohol reserve, as those blithe (but essential) guests never obey. Do supply both colour wines, but enforce preferential treatment of white wine drinkers if hosting on pale carpets. For spirits, attend to the basics first (vodka, gin, whisky, bourbon, rum), then think of frivolities. If you care to, prepare a few pitchers of cocktails; stick to one or two varieties. A fun bar encourages merriment, so provide some garnishes, proper glasses, ice and lots of mixers.

Simple Snacks

Food is alcohol's safety net; any sort of hungry hedonism usually ends in tears, fights and gutters. Cold, morsel-sized finger food is fine. The more instantly edible it is, the less mess (of various sorts) will be created. Prepare all snacks in advance and display in ample supply. Stack up napkins and plates and don't forget repositories for pips and scraps. Plan menus in affinity with the drunken need to carb-load and remember the law of diminishing returns: present your guests with a gastronomic panoply and they may well slump into postprandial contentedness. Situate your offerings in an area that allows plenty of access for drunk and hungry grazers. Don't hover but clear the debris occasionally; utilise friends (especially those looking lost) as gofers. Hiring a waitress grants instant entry into the superhostess league.

Checklist

Last minute tasks: arrange furniture to create dance floors for scene-stealers and dens for the sedentary, check that any atmosphere catalysts (think lighting and décor) are in place, put plenty of ashtrays out, prop the windows open, check that wine is open, lock secrets away (if necessary whole rooms). You should squirrel away any crystal glasses and prized vintages, particularly when hosting big benders. Line up a whole evening's worth of tunes, ensuring that there is enough choice for changes of heart, pace and taste. Mix in a few guilty-pleasure crowd pleasers and consider entrusting DJ duties to a friend keen to show off their decks. Rattling around in an empty space is a real atmosphere anaesthetic; enlist a few friends to arrive on time and help you get the party started.

Dinner Party

Dinner parties are sensitive little souls. When they go smoothly, there is no better way to spend an evening. Here, delicious foods, sparkling company and home comforts come together in cosy communion. It can be a real challenge to coordinate the dinner, drinks and social buoyancy, however, making the dinner party much more testing than its stand-up counterpart. Homeliness is key; snobbery will revolve around the menu and ingredients. Expect guests to happily squeeze around a breakfast bar for dinner, but dare to serve them granulated coffee and their smiles will quickly sour.

The food is not actually the most important thing, it's the company that matters. Your guests need you; don't be the galley slave all night. Stick to tried and tested 'here's one I prepared earlier' recipes (pies, stews, casseroles, bakes), matched to the sophistication of your audience. Respect vegetarians, religions and any guests fanatical about 'intolerances'. Don't subject all guests to a fruitarian or rare blood-type diet. Super-fresh, locally sourced or seasonal ingredients will please, as will colourful and pretty foods. Supply at least two courses; buying in pre-packed pud is quite acceptable. The result shouldn't leave guests feeling sick with excess or desperate to stop off for a takeaway on the way home (plenty of warm, fresh bread will fill most gaps). If you must fake the whole dinner, just come clean. People will only assume that a fraud in the kitchen is a fraud in life. Don't rely on guests to provide drinks. Stockpile a lot of everything including pre-dinner drinks (champagne?), digestifs and wine to accompany the food. Wise hostesses often have accounts with late-licence delivery services.

Only invite as many guests as can be seated *à table*; lap-dining is simply second-rate and any more than six for a nervy host is just a recipe for disaster. Hierarchical seating orders are far more suited to formal dinners and providing place cards will appear over-controlling unless feeding hundreds. With bijou dinner parties, hosts can let the seating plan fall naturally, though some guests will dither sheepishly until prodded into their designated seat. It may be wise to have a mental seating plan; use this to spice things up or avoid showdowns. Alternate boys and girls (or prepare to suffer football/shampoo monopolies), separate couples, park those who have similar interests together and use shy beta types to diffuse any domineering raconteurs. It is the host's prerogative to play cupid, but only with the lightest of touches. Older generations should be honoured (or compensated) with great seats. Your seat (and that of an unwitting attendant) should be nearest the kitchen door.

Do whatever you can in advance to allay stress. Lay the table as this will be the nerve centre of your evening. Keep it simple and spotless, or march to your own beat with charmingly mismatched crockery. Lay out two sets of glasses: one for wine and one for water. Hold by their stems to avoid fingerprints. Most diners are happy to recycle their cutlery from starters to mains; plates should be changed at each course. Fabric napkins are nice but anything is better than nothing. Draft in help if necessary and aim to serve food within an hour of guests arriving (a decisive time of arrival can help the horizontally inclined). Guests get cheesed off – and drunk – if made to wait too long.

Some vestiges of the old-fashioned rules remain. Ladies and oldies should be served first, you should be served last. Consider an uncoordinated start for foods that spoil fast; hot food must always be served on heated plates. It's perfectly acceptable for guests to serve themselves and pass dishes around. Service should always be snappy. Don't make your guests suffer without salt and pepper; don't take offence if any is requested. Delegate the wine pouring (unless you need to control a loose cannon's intake) and make sure water is quickly topped up. Always offer your guests second/third helpings and don't whip plates away until all eating has ceased. Mains should follow starters in a swift fashion but leave a nice long gap before pudding, before which all savoury paraphernalia is best removed. Round off with coffee or tea, pudding wine and port, and have a few games up your sleeve for any lasting or tricky conversational droughts.

House Guests

Visiting Time

'Do make yourself feel at home!' So goes the platitude, but it's a rare (and saintly) host that truly means it, and an egocentric guest that indulges it. What hosts really mean is that guests should just loosen up, but this doesn't extend to drinking straight from the carton and pottering about naked. Spending time in such close proximity uses up oxygen fast. It requires considerable diplomacy and a total suspension of all sulks and tempers (unless, of course, you don't want them to return ever again). Home turf does not bring home advantage; it's you and your tastes that are under inspection. Prior to your guests' arrival, therefore, it's advisable to fumigate the house and hide all your dirty secrets. It is wise to set some boundaries to thwart the plans of stray-dog guests; open invitations are most regrettable.

Scene-Setting

The expert hostess will ship in favourite foods and superior snackage. Breakfast is especially fun and multifarious and menus will suit even the pickiest eaters. The guest bedrooms must meet good B&B standards or higher. They will have crisp, clean sheets, two pillows or more per head, basic toiletries, towels (never flannel-sized), blankets, hangers and, for show, scented candles/flowers. Hosts of single bedroom endowment should not sacrifice their own bed. If they do, guests will feel either unduly comfortable (thus harder to uproot), or guilty (truly a terrible burden). Hosts should line up guest entertainments: games, walks, sports, pubs (but no compulsory early-morning workouts). Guests need directions and packing instructions; omit these and forever resent obliging them your wardrobe.

The Arrival

You should expect to receive a house gift. Grit your teeth; even the nastiest effort must be loved wholeheartedly. The unspoken code of hosting is to go slightly out of one's way in honour of one's guest. An enduring sense of self-sacrifice should be assumed but never be a martyr. Hospitality must be on tap – at least for the first day or so. Three square meals should be volunteered, plus elevenses, fourses and a nice cup of tea whenever seems appropriate. The sooner guests are invited to help themselves, of course, the sooner the burden is off you. Any offers of help should be rejoiced in – running a hotel is nil fun. Non-stop company can be exhausting, so know when to take time out. Guests often need to be treated like children; they should face neither suffocation nor neglect.

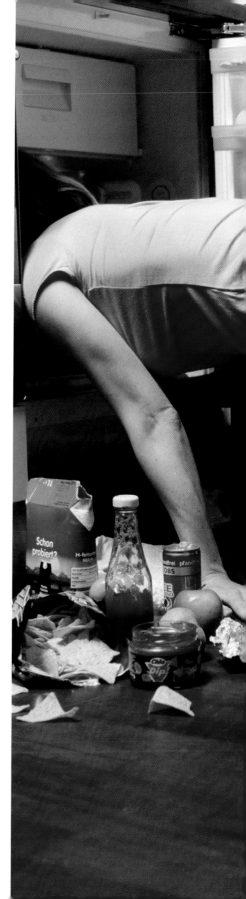

House Rules

To curtail inevitable awkwardness, at least some territory must be conceded. Show them around, to their rooms, the loo and offer to lend anything. Only at this point can you deliver the blow of house rules. If you can do this without making guests feel as though they're staying at a museum or a boot camp then establishing a loose structure can mean less gauche bumbling. As some of us are larks and some of us owls, it is the breakfast hour that can be the most confounding. Inform guests whether it is to be taken ensemble or whenever they care for it, otherwise face them cupping ears at doors and straining to gauge signs. Guests should never be harried out of bed, as bed time is so personal. If a guest behaves in a way that is annoying, a quiet word should embarrass them into behaving.

The Departure

Sleepover guests usually take the hint after a good fry-up and you can usually eject weekend guests after a nice roast – take note, guests. At some time or another, you will have to entertain an unannounced overnight guest (perhaps an incapacitated dinner guest, or a waif on your doorstep). Hosts should apply a sliding scale of hospitality, which can start at all-giving and happily slip once your guests start making nuisances of themselves. Once the comfort of tea and biscuits has been withdrawn, the outside world will begin to look more appealing. Those Who Pop In don't necessarily have to be welcomed. Use white lies – an appointment, a parental visit or simply a good hiding place – to put them off. Those who outstay their welcome should be dealt with directly (again, white lies are effective here).

Good Guest

To secure more invitations, ensure that you RSVP and then commit. Bailing out on the day is only acceptable if you are struck down with a tropical disease or an inexorable work/personal crisis; the host should be alerted to this as soon as possible. Respect the dress code but sparkle (it's good for you and good for the party). Bring at least one bottle (also good for you and good for the party). Even if abstaining yourself, it's polite to bolster the wine cellar.

Set yourself apart from more remiss guests by bringing nibbles, a house gift or champagne. If you are unlikely to return the hospitality, over-compensate here. Bringing flowers can create hassle for the host so offer to take the chore out of their hands. Arrival time gives a real insight into loyalty. Dependable friends arrive a few minutes after the

prescribed time (if it's 8 for 8.30, they are there by 8.30 at the latest). Under- or over-shooting the runway is both inconvenient and offensive; you should radio ahead in both cases.

The best guests readily climb down the rabbit hole and step right into the party groove, charming old and new friends with outrageous yarns and witty repartee, rescuing peripheral hoverers, and slyly mobilising static guests. Most parties appreciate naughty streaks. A little bit of mischief can add essential spice (but must never happen at the expense of feelings). More sensibly, you can consider a little altruism and volunteer to pour, chop or clean up. Always toast the host and compliment the chef; it's kinder to suffer grim food in silence (unless it is unfit for human consumption). If seated between the

living dead, only be convinced of your own fabulousness. If gatecrashing, ask your accomplice to call ahead. If you have no accomplice, be sure to bring plenty of extra charm.

Rather unfairly, being the last man standing is not considered the best look, while slipping out early to catch the rest of the circuit is somehow always hawkishly spotted. Leaving without due goodbyes to the host (unless helplessly incapacitated) is a black mark on the invitee spreadsheet. Other guests – your friends, those you hung out with, those who see you leave – should also be waved off. It's perfectly acceptable to interrupt their conversation to do so. The host-thanking ritual must continue into the next day, regardless of whether the party was hot or not. For casual dinners and parties, email or text is fine.

Bad Guest

Perhaps you think it would be more fun to get blacklisted? Follow these easy steps to social exclusion: call up your host beforehand and ask who else is coming, RSVP late (in order to keep your options open), don't reply at all. Better still, be the no-show and make it look like you had something better to do. For house parties, shun your duty to warm up the atmosphere and stay in a pub around the corner until closing time; only turn up when the party is in full swing. Wear downbeat clothes to flatten the atmosphere.

Arrive with the cheapest bottle of wine you can find, or with nothing at all (couples should bring no more than a bottle between them). If you insist on bringing a gift, make sure it's the box of chocolates that has been in constant circulation from party to party and is now well past its sell-by date. Be known as a desperate guest who would turn up to the opening of an eyeball. Arrive before the assigned time and don't call ahead to warn. Get in the host's way, demand their undivided attention and send them into a spin.

Alternatively, turn up late, drunk and with an unannounced entourage. Proclaim your newly adopted vegan habit only on arrival. Publicly criticise the host's methods; proceed to take over. Subject the host's wine to a hard-nosed tasting with all the snorting and gargling. In a non-smoking household, light up (over dinner, ideally) and treat the place like an ashtray. Decline all home-baked goods and demonstrably spit out distasteful foods. Drink your host out of house and home – selecting only the out-of-bounds premier cru – then fall asleep at the dinner table. Ignore any spillages. Insist on moving from your appointed place at dinner.

Start a catfight or introduce a highly upsetting topic of conversation. Hog the limelight, preferably with a torrent of tears. Turn on the TV and settle into the football highlights. Hit on off-limits people. Bang forcefully on the loo door and repeatedly turn the locked handle when waiting. Never consult the host before producing classified drugs. To cause maximum offence, bring out the naughty salt at the table in between courses; subject all to peer pressure (or worse, keep it all to yourself). Overstay your welcome and miss all the host's hints, then take to their bed. Reclaim your gift when you finally leave and steal a trophy for good measure. The next day, do nothing, nada, zip.

Flatmates

If there is only one way of doing things, go solo. If, however, you are hoping for access to a second wardrobe and the invitation to a join in on a pasta bake, a few golden rules must be observed. Prepare to share, be considerate and always be neighbourly. Sharing an inner sanctum is a precarious act. To protect friendships and ensure peace on the home front, a few more specifics must also be attended to.

If your policy of *laissez-faire* only amounts to the *laissez* and never the *faire*, you should consider a housework rota. Washing-up can't wait, so wash what you use. Don't be petty and wash up others' odds and ends. Domestics will arise over the simplest strike action. Your bedroom is yours to treat as you wish, but the communal areas are not. Don't let your jumble become part of the furniture, or leave flatmates with no choice but to nag.

Hogging the communal facilities – the phone, bathroom, sofa or washing machine – during their respective rush hours won't do your popularity much good. So, if in doubt, ask first.

Cooking meals together, or taking turns, is cooperative. If you prefer not to be tied in, consider the occasional random act of kindness; bake a cake or cook when your flatmate is too busy. Always veer towards the generous side when buying communal supplies. Don't help yourself to others' food, especially if it's unopened or is a luxury (and if you helped yourself, always replace it).

Don't let money become an issue. Be reliable, pull your weight, split the responsibilities and resist leaning on generosity/IOUs. Pass on all telephone messages (don't rely on your memory – write them down). Then (and only then) you can expect the same treatment in return from your flatmate.

Unless you are blessed with a sisterly relationship, always ask before borrowing. Your flatmate's room should be their secret and not your privilege. Any damage must be confessed to and instantly replaced. If you suspect that your flatmate isn't keen to share their things with you, don't push them.

Finding a stranger in residence on the sofa or, even worse, in your bed, is rarely a nice surprise. Do your flatmates the courtesy of asking permission when inviting friends to stay. With overnight guests, this should be merely academic but, with longer-term candidates, your flatmate's approval is imperative. You're responsible for providing your guest with any practicalities that they'll need (towels, toiletries, bedding). Guests are not licensed to bring their own friends back to yours.

If your boyfriend all but moves in, your responsibilities in the flat are not then halved, but are actually doubled. He should contribute practically and socially. Some over-compensation may be due, especially if any tensions from your flatmate are sensed.

Nothing overly social should be organised (no matter how last minute) without requesting the permission and company of your flatmate. If they can't make it, you should offer to reorganise. Likewise, all efforts should be made to attend your flatmate's gatherings. Not all socialising should be done at home.

Boundaries need to be established and social efforts need to be extended to maintain good flatmate friendships. Neither fester permanently in the flat, nor always be out (or, if you are, invite them along sometimes). If something's on your mind, don't harrumph or wait for the niggles to implode. Telegraph any concerns with some light ribbing or sensible discussions. But if it starts to go really wrong, save your friendship and move out.

N.B. if you're renting, then flatmates should have equal rights. If one of you owns the property, then big decisions and parties can only go ahead with the owner's complete say-so.

Girls have a tendency to blow the tiniest things out of proportion. Brush off small-mindedness. Don't eat their food, flirt with their boyfriends or copy their style. Boys' horizontal nature is great for peace but bad for housework. Install the rota; discuss rather than nag. Don't parade about nearly-naked and don't be territorial with their female guests. Try to compromise on TV tastes or, better still, invest in your own set.

A note on siblings. Familiarity tends to dissolve the veneer of manners, so the rules are even more important with siblings. Stick to the ground rules.

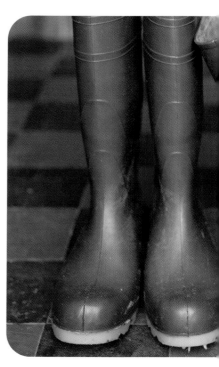

Country Guests

Usual rules don't apply to country life. Country weekends tend to require an altogether different manner and style, from one's dress to conversation and even dealing with the locals.

Since a country weekend largely revolves around the home, it is crucial to muck in, respect the house rules and, as privy to the intimacies of another's abode, be discreet. The host is king of their castle, and attention-seekers will be cut to size. An equilibrium of calm is striven for, and any metropolitan tastes for mobile phone/TV addiction or busy, maniacal behaviour won't guarantee a return invite.

The usual form is to arrive on Friday evening or Saturday morning, and leave after Sunday lunch (N.B. 'stay for lunch on Sunday, won't you?' means please leave soon afterwards).

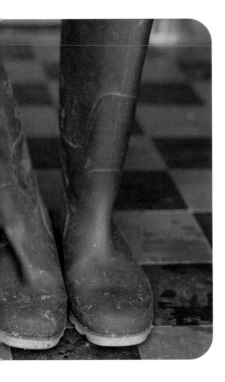

City dwellers must try to adapt to the restorative powers of life's simple pleasures. Sorties will be made to the Great Outdoors. Townies will quickly show themselves up if the countryside isn't respected. Don't drop litter, don't terrorise livestock and don't trample on crops. Leave gates as you found them and greet strangers (things are different in the countryside). A visit to the local pub is quite a field trip; any snobbery or sniggering towards regulars is a most unforgivable misjudgement. Concede their home advantage and endeavour to conform to their ways, but don't lay claims to their patch.

Urban wear never looks good in the wilderness; resolute homeliness is the way forward. Daywear should be comfy and muted in colour. Splashing out on all the kit – the flat cap, a Harris tweed three-piece, Fair Isle knits – makes you look like an amateur. It's traditional (and therefore on the wane) to dress up for dinner. Check with your host first, but a good rule is to dress according to the grandeur of the house. Make sure you acquaint yourself with the weekend's itinerary in advance as it's up to you to come prepared for activities. A lengthy yomp is compulsory at any time of the year, so bring robust walking shoes, waterproofs and plenty of warm layers. It's usually colder in old and rambling country piles, so be well prepared and strengthen your defences. Never ever grumble about being frozen.

Ruddy cheeks, windswept hair and the humiliation of new sports may hold little allure for indoorsy city types, but it really doesn't do to be the outsider. So, join in, assume some enthusiasm, and genuine enjoyment may follow. There is the added complication that the classic country pursuits (hunting, shooting and fishing) may collide with an urbanite's delicate tofu tastes. If so, it's perfectly acceptable to decline, but important to mention it before your arrival so that expensive bookings aren't wasted.

Expect all creatures great and small. Pets, farm animals and, with more open borders between man and nature, a wide range of creepy crawlies, furry and feathered things are to be expected (and accepted). If you're in possession of a four-legged friend, you must get permission from the host. Bear in mind that the countryside is a very different environment for little handbag-dwelling pavement-walking creatures. Also, in some households, animals often seem to have more rights than humans.

Face to Face

Introductions

And they're away. Introductions are the starter's orders to any social encounter. There are hurdles aplenty. There are complex hierarchical codes, tradition versus anti-tradition, memory blanks and lurking gaucheness. False starts are inevitable. While some people are not so good on first impressions, others may impress you with charm, only to disappoint on closer inspection.

The order of introductions is ruled by status. Always introduce to the most important people first: women, elders and high ranks. So, men are introduced to women ('John, this is Jane'), juniors to seniors and age pulls rank over sex. Individuals are introduced to the group first, then the group to the individual. For example, 'Tim, I'd like you to meet my friends James and Anne. Everyone, this is Tim'. Surnames are unnecessary.

Married couples should be introduced individually and not, say, as John and Jane Simpson, but it's useful to point out their link (e.g. mention that they are married). If you're the link between a group and a new arrival, it's up to you to handle the introductions.

Using someone's name is an instant bonus, but overuse will quickly begin to sound nauseatingly overfamiliar (as will premature nicknaming). Those with names like a mouthful of marbles will appreciate efforts to pronounce them, so ask if unsure. If someone is getting your name wrong, correct them. They will feel foolish if they find out later.

Forgotten their name? Try to blame the noise level, ask for a business card or check with someone else. If suffering a total blank, trigger your memory by asking what they're up to these days.

Admitting that you can't remember someone's name is a real slight. If an introduction to a third party is required, sidestep any memory loss by asking 'have you two met?'. Never ignore an introduction because a name fails you. Be sure to save face for others and introduce yourself if an introduction is failing to materialise.

Stuck for words? A good delivery demands charm and pace. Be succinct and clear. Add some humour to relax proceedings. Drop in some common-ground conversational prompts such as 'John's also a tiddlywinks champion'. If someone has a specific relationship to you, make it explicit: 'Susan's my tennis partner' or 'Peter's my milkman'.

'Hello, great to meet you' is a usual and perfectly acceptable response. The straight-bat greeting of 'how do you

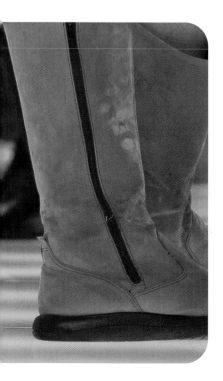

do' is business-like and old-fashioned. It's also a salutation, not a question so, if directed at you, the correct response is just to repeat it back. 'How are you?' is a rhetorical non-starter; 'I've heard so much about you' is disconcerting. Try to qualify it with a small conversation prompting detail: 'I hear that you've just returned from Timbuktu'.

Burning but boring questions such as 'what do you do?' or 'where do you live?' are unimaginative, tedious and can sound judgemental. Try to avoid them. If you are asked, be upfront and open. After all, you might discover that you've something in common with your new companion. Being cagey will only prompt suspicion.

N.B. only pass on business cards to new people if it's very relevant. Don't hand out willy-nilly.

Graceful Greetings

Aim for a firm, assured handshake. The hinge should be your elbow, not a limp wrist. Supplement with eye contact and a warm smile. Don't shake for too long and never with both hands. Do shake a bit, though, as total immobility can feel a bit spooky. Any bone-crunching, pumping or holding hands with a vice-like grip is saved for men with severe inferiority complexes. Nice girls remain feminine and self-assured, and those who are clammy of hand should wipe them (invisibly) first.

Social kissing is bound up in rules and doubts. A potential minefield, to kiss or not to kiss is usually dependent on age, background, profession, your relationship and, of course, your mood. The key is to be alert and scan for the potential recipient's intentions and to signal your own early on. Be decisive.

Stand back if you would rather not get affectionate, but if someone evidently wants to kiss, it would be outrageous to refuse. Don't just stand there rigidly; you must lean into it, even just a little bit. If you'd prefer to shake hands, be sure to hold yours out before any kissing manoeuvres begin.

When you kiss, bring the recipient in by putting an arm on their shoulder. Usually it's right cheek first, but prepare to change direction at the last minute (this is where it can get excruciating so decisiveness is key). If you are just going for a single kiss, pull back immediately or face that head shaking 'will we, won't we?' confusion. If a second comes by surprise, just go with it. N.B. no sound effects, air kissing or saliva traces. If you leave lipstick, then it's your duty to tell them. You actually

have to activate the kissing mechanism; merely holding cheek against cheek feels insincere and weirdly empty. Avoid kissing people in wide-brimmed hats or if you are both wearing glasses.

As a general rule, don't kiss people you don't know. If presented with a member of the older generation, allow them to take charge. Blundering in with a double hit could cause some alarm. Group-kissing often seems a bit hollow after the tenth. You can casually wave them all in or blow a kiss or two. With goodbyes, don't linger. Loitering is annoying when new conversations have begun, so when you've decided to make your exit, make sure you actually leave. For kissing, hand-shaking, hellos and goodbyes, be sure to get up from your parked position. Only administer hugs to close friends and family.

Clever Words

Conversation. Some people have the gift, while some don't. Do not fear, however, as the craft of conversation can easily be acquired.

Conversation is always supposed to be spontaneous, but a little homework can give you the advantage. So, read the newspaper, develop well-informed opinions and absorb trivia. Since the question 'how are you?' comes as no surprise, think of a colourful response. Be armed with interesting questions and, if prone to social blanks, adopt an *aide-mémoire* for boyfriends'/children's names (i.e. a note in the address book).

Charm isn't magic; it's just a series of components spruced up with a bit of empathy, tact and poise, aided by a bit of flirting and banter. Affect *bonhomie* and judicious optimism; be outrageous but never obnoxious. Ask questions but don't interview. Be interested and interesting; react to others' body language. When in a one-on-one, treat the other like the only person in the room. Talk and listen equally; make sure the talking and listening isn't just about you. If in a group, be inclusive but not egotistic, and invite stray sheep into the fold (i.e. 'we were just talking about…'). To join a group, make some eye contact, but don't disturb the flow.

Close friends should be able to ask each other Life's Big Questions, but until familiarity is manifest, all openers should be more indirect. Open-ended questions (i.e. the hows, whys, whats, wherefores) are more constructive than dead-end questions that require only a yes/no response. Subject matter is best if generalised or observational – never be too intrusive.

Some say that small talk is boring, simplistic and cringe-making, but often it's a necessary preamble to flowing, unscripted conversation. Most people don't mind idle chit-chat about relatives, food, the news and décor.

Remember that no one's interested in the weather; it's always a universal metaphor for dull, boring conversation. In times of dire need, however, it is an instant social facilitator. Hopefully, by the end of a discussion on how sunny, rainy or frosty it's been, a considerably more interesting topic for conversation will have been found.

Likewise, the question 'how are you?' does not fire the imagination. It can be a green-light for whingers and self-obsessed windbags. Among good friends, however, it is a very important social cushion, the inevitable prelude to asking more meaningful and personal questions.

Greet enemies with basic courtesy and then gracefully extricate yourself. Don't let them ruin your conversational charm so, if words suddenly fail you, invent a contact lens drama, suddenly spot a long-lost friend across the room or pretend that a 'very important call's coming through'. Ensconce yourself in a deep corner far away to avoid any further eye contact. Any confrontations should be conducted privately.

Conversational Quicksand

Political Correctness

Unless you are in tried and well-tested company, any kind of extreme opinion – think gender, money, class, religion, race, disability, sexuality, baldness or size – is always risky.

Tediously, it's advisable to temper extreme opinions and words like 'hate'. Think twice before raising taboos and never make sweeping generalisations. Note that double standards apply; it's fine for minorities to send themselves up but it's less fine for anyone else.

If you're insulted by someone else, consider selective deafness to brush it under the carpet. If you wish to react, try firing off a witty comeback. It's most satisfying and will often diffuse tension. Don't be too reactive to other people's opinions. Making some allowances for freedom of speech or humour is more sociable than a moralising sermon.

Foot-in-Mouth Disease

The loose of tongue face a big, gaping trapdoor; spoken words are impossible to retract and a delicate patch-up job is called for. You must apologise at once – 'I'm sorry, that came out all wrong' – and try to blame nerves or confusion. Showing embarrassment will make your remorse more convincing, and inviting your victim to laugh at you is a very effective leveller. Don't keep on digging; gracefully and smoothly divert attention on to pastures new.

Certain subjects induce distress if raised inappropriately. Avoid death and divorce. Don't ask strangers if they are married or have children (or if not why not). Never launch off on one about illness as you will risk causing serious offence/embarrassment. In most cases, some quick backtracking or a prompt apology is then demanded of you.

Nosiness

Licence to pry increases with familiarity. Always precede with 'do you mind me asking…'. Fudge if necessary. Try 'what do you think about counselling?', rather than 'are you having therapy?'. Ask the closely guarded after they have had a dose of alcohol. Beguile nosy parkers by turning the question back on them. If cornered, maintain a dignified silence, or tell them to mind their own business.

Age is often a matter of curiosity. It is more acceptable to ask your subject if they are younger than you, are male or are drunk. If asked to guess, then flatter by shaving a few years off your estimate (except for under-21s craving maturity). If you're asked but don't want to answer, then evade or humorously refuse to respond. Being caught lying is almost twice as humiliating as being considered antiquarian.

Conflict Management

Arguments are a bit like sport. There is a rush of adrenaline, followed by rallies and volleys, along with footing to lose and a victory to win. They can be fun, but to spew abuse, storm off or throw missiles is automatic defeat. Never say harmful things or break confidences in anger. Hysteria clouds judgement and will bring public shame. Once you're at the screaming match stage, any mutual respect will be obliterated. Things may escalate in a flash, but vicious anger can cause long-term damage and require a painful repair job.

Listening without interrupting and weighing up both sides of the case is a successful method of undermining your opponent. The emotionally incontinent, the totally uninformed and those with a minority view should think very carefully before stepping into the ring.

Awkward Silences

There can be reward in the challenge of successfully warming up a dormouse or laconic misanthrope. It might be hard work, but invest some time, ask open-ended questions or widen the group. Scan your surroundings for any obvious cues, for example unusual architecture, or awful music. Consider plumbing your knowledge of current affairs ('I was just reading that…'). A slightly ridiculous or stilted conversation is better than none at all. Learn to love a silence and don't feel the need to fill every pause. Know when to quit – ten minutes is usually charity enough.

If, however, silence is accompanied by a pair of tightly pursed lips, you may have caused offence. Smooth over the comment and introduce a new topic of conversation sharpish. Don't misread dislike for shyness.

Tools of Conversation

How do you prevent conversation from descending into vacuity? Take the high-risk road. It will usually pay off; thrilling conversationalists are social magnets. Engaging on such a level requires the lightest of touches and a scattering of sweeteners to subtly indicate that your intentions are benign.

Ribbing should be employed as a reciprocal strategy; a ping-pong game of good-humoured fun-poking. It can create a certain cushioned directness that makes for closer bonds. N.B. boys are much readier recipients, exercise caution with very girly-girls and avoid humiliating anyone.

The elephant in the room (i.e. any unspeakable matter preying on both minds) can create terrible tension. For example, can they actually remember my name? Have they been seeing my boyfriend? If something is bothering you, it can only be resolved by daring to speak of it. An oblique approach is best in delicate situations; touch on the subject and open the opportunity for discussion. Park the topic when you see the brick wall looming and avoid that car-crash conversation. If you are being hammered at to open up, let them know early on and firmly if it's off-limits and then change the subject.

Shock tactics break down barriers, but a lively debate can be disastrous. Whilst strong opinion is usually well received amongst peers, controversy is most unwelcome in unknown company. Go easy with challenges on those who are younger or more shy than you. If you are in such a position, don't allow your feathers to be ruffled. Any tears or losing one's temper can cause untold hassle and loss of respect.

When you're about to be especially blunt, apologise in advance – 'forgive my honesty...' or 'sorry for labouring the point...'. Like silencing a gun just before firing a bullet, the point remains intact but the aggression is muted.

Well-played praise disarms all but the most unyielding of battleaxes. The power of flattery undermines the most rigorous of mental border controls. It can get you off on the right foot with someone, or can distract others from any blunders or premature departures. Flattery can be a useful prompt for the conversation, and buttering up the vain can bring people round to your way of thinking. Compliments don't need to be true to be convincing. Don't go over the top or be cloyingly insincere. Your quota per conversation is really just one or two; any more is gushing. Note that telling someone that they look fantastic when really they just look normal will seem false and could upset them with thoughts of how grim they must have looked on previous meetings.

Sharing secrets connects people. It creates trust, deeper friendships and a whole reservoir of new secrets. Alcohol is an effective catalyst, but be cautious of exaggerated truths and emotional outpourings. Note: broken secrets lead to broken friendships.

Traditionally, girls are the joke when it comes to telling gags. Having your own repertoire of easy, cute numbers provides an excellent backup plan for when you're lumbered with the dreary. Humour can be a trusty backstop in some of the most awful of situations, but maintain standards and avoid any Christmas cracker jokes.

People are remarkably coy about walking away from one-on-ones. There is a fine line between rudely cutting it short and lingering on, stretching out the conversation. Thankfully, some exit lines don't require utterance. Take the coat trick as an example. You can signal your imminent planned departure by slowly packing up your bag and then putting on your coat. Companions will hopefully mirror your bold actions and, before you know it, it's done. If you are trapped at a party, be direct but lace your parting words with compliment: 'well, it was really interesting talking to you'. If less confident, you can invert it: 'I'm sure I'm boring you...', 'I mustn't monopolise you'. If you must make an excuse to escape, make it 'needing the loo' not 'getting a drink' as they may ask for one too. You can also consider 'suddenly' catching sight of someone you need to talk to 'urgently', but this tactic needs to be executed with style and tact. If you are just struggling to interrupt when you genuinely want to get another drink or need the loo, the line, delivered with a smile and some eye contact, is 'hold that thought…'.

Troublesome Talk

Arrogance

To steamroll one's own opinions may afford quick control, but once others come to realise that it's a case of might over right, glory is very short-lived. Self-promotion only looks amateur; those who are intimate with success know to underplay their genius. Try cutting the arrogant down to size with a little bit of teasing, or even imagine them naked, and you'll find it easier to cope with them. Exercising modesty may protect you from hubris, but if you are too self-effacing, people will only want to give you a bit of a slap.

Name-dropping and bragging can have the opposite of the desired effect. Instead of impressing others, it will only show up the perpetrator as someone empty and status-anxious enough to need weak, artificial and shameless devices to try and impress others.

Bores and Lightweights

Bores are excellent companions if you are dying for a rest from talking, but otherwise tiresome. If you're stuck with someone as riveting as photosynthesis, then rib them for rabbiting on, grab a few allies, or carefully redirect the focus elsewhere. An 'accidental' interruption will prevent them from finishing. It's a public service to stem the domination of insufferable bores.

Comments such as 'we must go out for a drink. I'll call you' will translate as 'there's more chance of you being adopted by aardvarks'. So, if you're prone to such hollow phrases, consider 'it was really lovely to see you' instead. While being perfectly pleasant, you won't leave anyone waiting by the phone, or leave yourself looking very insincere. But if you do suggest having lunch, be sure to follow up.

Foreign Usage

There's nothing wrong with a broad vocabulary or a bit of *je ne sais quoi*, but always strive for linguistic elegance. You should respect your audience, so using obscure words at the bus stop will only have you relegated to the try-hard set. Conversation is not a competition, and no one ever appreciates alienation by intellectual one-upmanship. Be totally sure you're certain of a word's meaning. Any foreignisms should be anglicised in pronunciation. Unless you are speaking to a native, rolling r's and the like will be seen as pretentious.

Unclear business-use phrases are very grating: 'let's step up to the plate, give the heads-up and push the envelope on this one'. Likewise, Manhattan mouth – 'I'm going to have her call you on your cell' – anywhere east of New York State sounds wrong.

Ignorance

Do you admit or just bluff? It's situation and subject-dependent. If you are well out of your depth at a dinner party and are being subjected to the arrogance of a talking encyclopaedia, taking them on might well lead to more trouble and humiliation than it's worth. Keep quiet. In less gruelling circumstances, you can be more upfront and ask questions. If you're hoping to bluff your way and are asked your opinion, a vague answer can deflect the query. Looking at your feet and being shifty says 'ignorant' in no uncertain terms. Being caught out is far more compromising than admitting unscholarliness.

Don't even bother indulging your esoteric references in less informed circles, or drawing attention to others' ignorance. It's just a cheap (and cruel) trick for self-promotion.

Gossip, Bitching, Lies and Excuses

It seems unjust that gossip is taboo. It's actually very important for information exchange, status marking and bonding. It is an efficient means of defining what is (and isn't) socially acceptable and is also fairly enjoyable. Likewise, bitching gets frowned upon. Moralists claim that you should never utter words that you wouldn't say to someone's face. This attitude, however, could result in great rudeness. It denies the true rationale of bitching: the ability to offload onto a ready ear.

The best gossip is always the most dangerous. Guarding the secret should be one's goal but, if it's burning a hole (as they are prone to do), tell someone who's very far removed from the action. Take heed that confidences become especially breakable when intoxicated. Spreading muck that is patently untrue or unfavourably twisted is gratuitous and wrong. Those who peddle gossip and bitch incessantly get a reputation for being small-minded. Gossip is often born out of resentment, bitterness or jealousy – a reassuring rationalisation if you become a victim of it.

The occupational hazard of gossip is being overheard. Rule number one: watch your back. If you are totally sure you've been overheard bad-mouthing someone, try to remember your words. If nothing explicit was said, apologising will only rub the stain in. If you know that umbrage was taken, apologise at once. It you're too spineless to do it in person, email.

We are programmed to eavesdrop, so some personal slurs will inevitably be heard. Steel yourself and if there is any chance of overriding such instincts, do so. Block it out, walk away or alert the busybodies to your presence by coughing or suchlike. Inviting gossips to dig their own grave (i.e. letting them rant and then letting them know you've heard everything) may embody a kind of natural justice, but retribution only brings awkwardness. It's level pegging in the small-mindedness stakes; rise above it. If you care to confront any scurrilous gossip about you, try to deal with it at source. Stay calm – tantrums will only supply them with fresh material for the next round.

Every day, we all tell a few lies. The spectrum spans from dainty white to dirty black, via yellow (cowardly), purple (embroidered truths) and grey (casual workplace deceptions). For some, any lie is immoral; for most, lies can have a positive role. For example, they can sex up a story, or protect others' feelings. So while good girls don't lie, nice girls tell perfect untruths – i.e. ones that will be beneficial and that can never be discovered. Telling the odd (harmless) lie is justifiable, but living on lies forces others to distrust your every word.

The key to a good lie is to keep it simple, involve no one else and tell as few people as possible. If a lie just slips out, it's best to issue a disclaimer ('OK, so I'm exaggerating...') than for your audience to suspect you or catch you

out. One single exposé is enough to cast doubt on all your stories. Situations that require continuous lies (all of which require remembering) start to tangle up into a horrible web of deceit which will eventually trip you up. Remembering your tracks can become a complete headache and the guilt will nibble away at your conscience – and that's before the shame of being rumbled. Honesty may take courage, but it will save you from dishonour.

There are two choices when you are in conversation with a pathological liar: either ignore it all and quietly apply the 'divide by three rule', or confront them (your options mostly depend on your relationship with the fibber). A close friend should be ready for a 'come off it!'. Any challenge should be made in private and framed with good humour.

Fundamentally, excuses are lies, so the same rules apply. Too much detail and too many reasons only make things implausible and harder to remember. Feeding good friends a line is cowardly, and being caught out is normally worse than suffering the obligation in the first place. Any excuse must be rigorously thought through and memorised. Don't make excuses that falsely blame others without their permission. False doctors' appointments can be useful, thanks to our overriding sense of privacy – no one likes to push for details. Toothache is a compelling excuse (just clutch the chin), but migraines and food poisoning have lost all credibility.

The Written Word

Invitations

An invitation must seem inviting (i.e. a great occasion, a promising location), but it must also be informative. It lets guests know what's involved, who the hosts are, the nature of the occasion, the venue (send a map if necessary), the timings, what to wear, what to expect (and whether to expect nibbles or a sit-down meal), what to bring, if they can bring an ally and how (and if) to RSVP. The invite may be brimming with fabulously generous spirit, but trip up on any of these details and you'll spoil the gesture. Guests may get annoyed if they expected dinner, and embarrassed if they have to enquire.

An engraved stiff card shouts big production; a group email says informal huddle. Tradition/extravagance should be reserved for historic events such as weddings or big birthdays.

The traditional invitation is bound up in regulations, right down to proper dimensions/thickness, and even the correct positioning of the guest's name (top left, in fountain pen). The wording allows no concessions to humour or personality. 'At Home' parties tend to sound middle-aged and anyone born after 1970 is likely to scoff at such an affectation (N.B. traditionally 'At Home' invitations only come from hostesses). Displaying invitations like trophies on the mantlepiece doesn't make you look really popular.

The modern invitation is thankfully more liberal. The choice of style and presentation is vast. Electronic invites are very popular and make RSVPing far easier; some sense of occasion will be sacrificed since receiving anything of interest by post is always a rare treat. An actual invitation kick-starts a bigger sense of anticipation. Whereas written invitations rely on an accurate/up to date address book, email can be a far more effective party-rallier. News may spread virally – not always a bad thing. For big parties or gatherings, however, protect people's privacy by putting the addresses in the bcc box. Inviting by text is a yet more casual and modest medium. If inviting people by phone, don't expect guests to turn up on the right day, at the right place or even turn up at all, unless you follow up with written details or ring and remind them nearer the time. Never invite in person in front of people you aren't including.

Couples, if married, engaged or living together, should be invited as a pair. Apply a blanket rule for less official/permanent couples (i.e. all or nothing; not just the other halves of your favourite people).

Do not throw your towel on to the sunlounger before sunrise by asking for excessively advance commitment for casual events. Think a week or two in advance (not three months) for drinks or dinner parties. You should give more warning for summer/Christmas parties and catered events (at least six weeks is safe). At least three weeks in advance is best for birthday parties; spontaneity compromises turnout.

Always RSVP (unless you're actually instructed otherwise). Note that friends have certain duties to perform. Having to be prompted deserves a serious telling-off. Reply as soon as you can. If you won't know whether you can make it until nearer the time, then say so. A 'maybe' must be qualified, but if you can't go, don't flounder for an excuse.

The reply should be in an equivalent format to the invitation – i.e. formally or informally, by post, email or telephone. Never drop out of a commitment; if it must be cancelled, however, due reason and sufficient grovelling is imperative. Simply not turning up is unforgivable.

Formal responses should always be handwritten in fountain pen, preferably on headed paper or a nice card. Anti-traditionalists may be tempted to stray from the official template of referring to yourself in the third person but, in fact, its purpose is for speed. The RSVP can be quickly processed by the host (or their retinue of staff).

There is, therefore, some standard wording that should be used for formal invitations. An acceptance reads: 'Miss Victoria Blah-Blah thanks Mrs Simon La-di-Dah for her kind invitation to dinner to celebrate her 30th birthday on Friday 9th October and has much pleasure in accepting'. A refusal would read: 'Miss Victoria Blah-Blah thanks Mrs Simon La-di-Dah for her kind invitation to dinner to celebrate her 30th birthday on Friday 9th October, but much regrets she is unable to attend'.

Essential Stationery

Receiving a thoughtfully penned letter from a thoroughly modern girl should command delight. The impact is lost, however, if a piece of photocopier paper with the scrawl of a biro is extricated from a business envelope featuring the logo of an employer. Every sophisticate should have a stationery supply and stationery, like clothing, is an interface to personality.

The classic lady dutifully attends to the inventory of a traditional bureau. Writing paper should be watermarked, A5-sized, white/off-white in colour and a minimum of 100 gsm in weight. The letterhead should include your address, telephone number and email; never include your name. Letterheads should be engraved if affordable, otherwise go for flat-printed; thermographic printing looks cheap and is never a good idea.

Correspondence cards are the size of a postcard, 300 gsm, and include your name, mobile number and email; just the thing for brief notes and informal thank-yous.

Envelopes, sized to fit the writing paper or cards, should have diamond flaps. You can also invest in a set that's hand-lined with tissue paper for special occasions and special people.

This traditional kit requires financial outlay, and showy letterheads aren't to everyone's taste, after all. Unless you're corresponding with the Queen or other dynasties, a little colour and character is usually well-received. Hand-milled paper, homemade cards, airmail paper, graph paper, vintage postcards; the choice is yours. A random assortment of different-sized envelopes might be useful with such a kit.

Build up a collection of emergency birthday cards for last minute panics; stash away a selection to suit all ages and genders. Such cards should, of course, really be bought to match the person. Stamps should always be first class and never stuck on wonky.

Real ink, only in blue or black, is the traditional medium. It is still considered the finest; other colours are acceptable to those with contemporary tastes, but red is thought of as aggressive. Some more exotic colours can be difficult to read. Biros, felt-tips and pencils are deemed sloppy, but are defensible if artfully employed.

Computer-printed *communiqués* look horribly businessy and impersonal. An old-fashioned typewriter can lend charm, but always ensure you pen the actual signature.

Written Communications

The Perfect Letter

A delightful reverse up the information superhighway, letter-writing is enjoying a comeback. Letters should read as if the writer is sitting beside the reader: bubbling over with conversation. Order your thoughts before committing them to paper. Watch spelling and grammar; a thorough proofread is crucial.

Letter paraphernalia should include your address, the date (in full is nicely retro) and warm greetings; 'Dear...' or 'Dearest…' and never 'To'. The sign-off will match your relationship with the recipient. For older generations, bow to formality, i.e. 'Best wishes' ('Yours sincerely' and 'Yours faithfully' should be left for business correspondence). Ensure the recipient is correctly styled.

Avoid P.S. bombshells. A postscript should never be too heavy and should not be tagged on to solemn missives.

Presentation

Letters are keepsakes, so a little bit of neatness will give a letter that chance of permanence. A doctor's scrawl has little allure and is quite inconvenient to decode. Layout should be straight and well-spaced (use an underlay sheet if prone to sloping off to one side), with new paragraphs for new ideas. A letter needn't be totally showroom-perfect; a correction is endearing if it's neatly and lightly executed. Anything scratched out or Tippexed is ugly and suspicious. Re-write if it gets dog-eared, riddled with mistakes or coffee/tear-stained.

Letters can be read over and over again, so think very carefully before you send anything too confessional/stormy. Sending letters with no purpose to any friends who live nearby is considered a bit odd, especially if you socialise with them regularly.

Thank You Letters

As an endangered species, most hosts or donors are pleased with any kind of recognition, be it a text, email, card or letter. While a text message is fine for a casual dinner, a lovingly handwritten letter is more suitable for a diamond ensemble. To overstate gratitude (e.g. a written note for a cup of tea) looks very desperate or insincere.

A thank you letter should be warm, witty and to the point. Start by saying how much you loved your X, Y or Z; not liking it should have no bearing on the act. Recipients of money should never express the quantity. Those blessed by a shower of gifts must personalise each letter, as production-line jobs can be so obvious. Thank you letters should be dispatched within a week, though it is never too late. Also, when in doubt, a written note is always well received.

Correct Cards

Some selflessness should be employed when writing postcards, so no bragging about the endless hours you've spent luxuriating in turquoise waters. Lay on the wit and charm; don't recycle the same old message to mutual friends.

Christmas cards are an efficient way of keeping in touch with people. 'Dear X, Happy Christmas, from Y' is a waste of paper and postman miles. It implies that the recipient is but a mere tick on your spreadsheet, so personalise each and every message.

Christmas circulars smack of self-praise. If a personal telephone call or face to face catch-up is impossible (i.e you're shackled to five children or stuck in Siberia), then a newsletter might be defensible. Send them out cautiously; much better to hand-write a few lines of news to those far away friends.

Letters of Condolence

Dilly-dallying is very inappropriate here. Letters should be written promptly (by hand and never by email). Phone calls are reserved for very close friends.

The letter should acknowledge the loss, include the deceased's name and a sincere expression of sympathy. An anecdote (only if they were personally known to you) is usually well received. The tone should be genuine and warm, not over-sentimental or hysterical. Keep it brief; a short paragraph will suffice. This isn't an opportunity for you to indulge in your prose-writing skills. The sign-off should also be duly respectful.

Writing a letter of condolence isn't an easy exercise, but the simplicity of sentiment will be much appreciated. N.B. only offer to help the bereaved if it is appropriate, you know them well and you're genuinely willing.

Email

The root of most email offence is time, or lack of it. We are busy and lazy; we like a shortcut so our mantra becomes 'that'll do'. An email sent in haste risks being polluted with unintended insult. Email vernacular is less considered than the written word, but we are inclined to say in an email what we couldn't say face to face. While email is wonderfully convenient, it is also an effective means of avoidance. Don't forget to talk too.

There's no mystery to writing good emails; just try to view it through the eyes of the receiver and read it through before sending. Always check carefully who is in the 'to' box.

Bother with the 'subject' box. If you are replying to old emails with a new topic, don't settle for the 'Re: Re: Re:' thread, and delete all the detritus that has gone before – make it just like new.

Be fastidious about name spelling. For example, is it Jon or John? Watch the length; two words is much too short, but a treatise is too long. Top and tail *communiqués* with salutations; dear or hello; thanks where thanks are due; bye, best wishes, kiss-kiss. Follow your correspondent's lead if available.

Writing proper sentences (and complete words), capitalising titles and ensuring good grammar and spelling will command respect. Remember that text in capital letters reads like you are shouting, while lower case overload will look lazy.

A little humour is a useful tool, but be cautious of sarcasm. Emoticons may be effective pointers, but are generally considered to be immature so try to avoid them. Exclamation marks have a little more credibility, but use sparingly.

Size, sense, 'to', top and tails, and tone must be checked before hitting 'send'.

Avoid chain emails; and assess your recipients for awareness issues or jokes. Never send unsolicited mega-emails; keep to 1MB max. Avoid hitting 'reply all' except for organisational purposes.

If you are very busy, be apologetic but not dismissive. Take a moment to write something; few recipients will be charmed by three-word 'how are you?' emails that deflect all efforts to communicate onto the recipient.

Response time must be within two days. Unless the conversation has quite obviously expired, it's friendly to keep the rally going. Response time politics is a spectrum from very keen to aloof. An instant reply is honest but impulsive and not recommended with boy-mails; 24 hours means it's been worked on

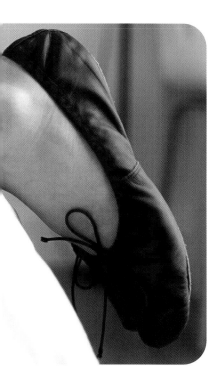

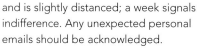

and is slightly distanced; a week signals indifference. Any unexpected personal emails should be acknowledged.

Before taking offence at abrupt or impertinent dispatches, remember the usual lack of deliberation that goes into an email. What may read as rather fresh is often sent entirely in good humour.

Emails provide no privacy. Beware of people reading over your shoulder, insecure servers and IT departments. Emails can also be read over and over again. They're traceable, so never say anything you couldn't defend. Always take a moment before hitting 'send' in anger; delete any rashness. Ditto with sending love-mails.

If you send an email to the wrong person, hit 'recall'. Then immediately phone them; try to grovel or persuade them to ignore/destroy it.

Getting Ahead

Office Politics

It's worth being cynical here. Bowing to the queen bee and supporting fellow worker bees pays dividends. Unless you are eking out a career in data input, or working a lonely graveyard shift at the crematorium, a little office cheer brings going-home time all the more near.

Offices are like families. Most are dysfunctional and all will have their own mother/father-knows-best routine. You will score points by conforming to an office's working model. For example, take 20-minute lunches, leave domestic and emotional dramas at home, keep social phone chat to a minimum and get in the rounds at post-work drinks. Persistent rebellion will alienate, but careful luck-pushing can be respected as spirited wilfulness. Compliance will only get you so far; mastering (and also playing up to) the game theory of your office and industry will surely advance your career trajectory.

Dress up to your ambitions. Being smart is strategic and, unless employed in solitary confinement, IQ loses impact without professional-looking clothing to match. Seductive dressing is very counterproductive. Girls who wear very short skirts, skirts with splits to where legs end, sheer fabrics or gaze-fixingly low-cut or cropped tops are not taken seriously, are talked about behind their backs and make themselves potential targets of harassment.

Professionalism should be switched on when you are within the office radar. Pick yourself up – be cool, courteous, focused and loyal to your employer, even if every last breath is faked. Plenty of favours will be reaped from forming alliances with others further afield (post boys, reception, security); redistribute perks and gifts to them. Respect the pecking order, the olds and those with more company years than you. Brazen ambition and trampling on toes tends to put noses out of joint.

Email and phone are the conduits of office politics. Email is the best tool for communicating with the important people and insures against any poorly timed interruptions. It is a useful device for discretion and distancing. Any slight delay in response can infer a necessary less-than-delirious interest, without the need to say as much (the antidote to which is picking up the phone). When it matters, you must respond immediately or, if you are pressed for time, send a holding email promising a response in due course. Those who have lost their mug, or similar trivia, should not invade communal email space to ask after it; to use 'reply all' is even more amateur. Telephonic interruptions should never be treated as such; always feign sheer delight to hear from your caller. If you are too busy, explain politely and not with a rushed brush-off. Always make sure you fulfil promises to return calls.

Always be discreet. Shouting down juniors is embarrassing for them, your witnesses and, most of all, you. Even if a public outing is deserved, spectators tend to sympathise with the underdog, not the aggressor. Check your temper; cool-headedness has much more sway (and less hubris). Pulling rank is so flaky. If necessary, calm criticism has far more impact. Never discuss salary with your colleagues. Someone (you, maybe) will always feel short-changed.

Respect confidentiality. Keep things to yourself when necessary and resist the temptation to pass on any sensitive information (professional or personal). Illicit material spreads like wildfire so talk with caution within the office walls. If you really can't help yourself, ensure that the finger can't be pointed at you. Beware of gossip. The office telegraph system is a key team-bonding tool and unofficial appointments board, but hard core gossips are presumed to be untrustworthy. Truths get diluted and secrets can get into the wrong hands or, the horror, right back into the subject's. Do not swallow (or pass on) unquestioningly.

Email is only one click away from going public, intentionally or otherwise (that email about A can end up going to A instead of the intended B). Check and double check recipients. Delete all serious evidence and check your 'sent items' and 'trash can'. Appropriate a cipher and give nosy IT departments the slip by switching to webmail (check with caution during office hours). Never use work email for anything that could be incriminating or highly personal. Above all, use your discretion and try not to be the subject of gossip.

Office Survival

Popularity counts on the ground and a few pleasantries oil the machine and get colleagues on side. Just a 'hello' when you see colleagues and perhaps a little social proactivity in the canteen will do it (N.B. office social kissing is unsuitable except perhaps before or after long leave). Those who ask learn faster, so communicate, but keep a lid on the whingeing – it is work, after all.

Share sweets, perks and ideas (and give people credit for their ideas). It's a simple model of give-and-ye-shall-get. Always include the Quiet Colleague in group emails. Credit in the bank of tea rounds accumulates interest fast. Ask before borrowing anything; make sure it stays borrowed and doesn't drift into possession. With whip-rounds, tip off donors as to what is expected (and if in doubt what to volunteer, just ask and

match). Tacit guilt trips help raise funds (in person and not by email) but must be presented as an option rather than an obligation. Who's responsible for remembering birthdays? Often no one, so take note and avoid favouritism.

Respect thy neighbours. Keep the volume down and silence your mobile. Don't eat stinky meals at your desk. If you inexplicably laugh out loud at your screen it's polite to share the joke, and neighbours should always get first dibs on sweets. When desk-hovering, be very subtle if you're copping a look at others' screens. Slinking away from paper jams is a core contravention of the code of neighbourly love.

Tardiness rarely goes unnoticed. If the company policy on presenteeism is reasonably liberal, always communicate any 'appointments' to the PA of the

boss (a useful ally as they'll decide if the boss needs to know). Forward plan sickies so colleagues aren't left in a fix (N.B. food-poisoning and migraines equal hangover or extended holiday; doctor's appointment equals interview). Struggling in when sick will sometimes win you some points, but never if you're contagious. Any illnesses are best explained to bosses directly to avoid rumour or the 'sick note' tag. The odd evening sacrificed to the office is good to have on account for trading in with impromptu duvet days.

When in meetings, switch off your mobile (not just to the silent setting) to eliminate checking for new missives or mistimed disturbances. Take some brief notes – it looks good and can prolong concentration. Never yawn and don't hog all the biscuits.

Office Romance and Sleaze

Pros and Cons

Pros: he may be the Chosen One. Illicit trysts are a great thrill and the desire to impress is motivating. A romantic bond may bring great teamwork; colleagues will be thankful for water-cooler fodder.

Cons: it's hugely distracting. There's no escape; proximity is misleading. Any tensions will be publicly observed. You will be the number one subject of small talk, truths will be embroidered and, if it all fails, you'll have to face the carcass daily. You may get dumped (at work) or, worst-case, you may even get fired.

The balance is tipped. Office flirting can catalyse productivity; office love is like dropping a big boulder into a small pond. The long-term forecast should show great rays of promise to justify the fallout. Many a true love has been discovered at work – signing a contract shouldn't require a vow of chastity.

Private or Public

Going public is only an option once *amour* has become regular reality. Any incubating romance requires full-time protection. All arrivals and departures must be carefully stage-managed and emailing is always preferable to furtive courting in dark corners. If you really must engage, stairs are often deserted in lift-serviced offices (and provide an exit strategy where lovers can scuttle off in separate directions).

If suspicions are aroused, your personal workstation may be searched, so always close down revelatory screen windows and use webmail. If love does blossom, a well-timed and diplomatic newscast to colleagues and the boss may bring blushes, but to deny all can make them feel alienated (N.B. check the small print to make sure that an office affair isn't a sackable offence).

Forbidden Love

Any romance more complex than the single-on-single *amour* dare not speak its name. If your paramour is married, it's essential to keep this secret *entre vous*. Colleagues could take the moral high ground while simultaneously spreading the muck far and wide. No rendezvous is secure within a five-mile radius of the office; take nun-like care at office gatherings as inhibitions become drowned by drink.

Equally dangerous is bonking the boss, which may be slammed as pure, naked ambition. Any promotion, even if well deserved, will be resented. Your affair must always be kept secret, even post-split. Any leaked information will be like a drop of blood in a piranha pool and will change everything. Even worse is entertaining intentions on your boss's partner: career suicide.

Estrangement

When romance turns sour (we told you so), be mature. High emotion must be banished; switch to autopilot. If the river of tears cannot be stemmed, take some leave. Knee-jerk resignations are regrettable; give it time and see if you can conquer the cringe phase. Confide in colleagues who were complicit. After all, cathartic confiding might facilitate your recovery.

When you are pursued by admiring colleagues, be cautious and err on the chaste side. Your career will never ever benefit from giving romantic charity to male colleagues. Even if you've already named your fantasy love children, such behaviour will muddy your prospects and reputation. Good excuses: perhaps you don't care to mix business and pleasure or, even if a little white lie, you can easily be happily spoken for.

Handling Harassment

Unfortunately there will always be pervs about, no matter what protective legislation is put in place. If any charm offensive turns offensive, be it physical or verbal, a sliding scale of intervention may be applied.

In uncertain beginnings, it's wise to keep it between you and him (or her). Untold complications may ensue with the introduction of a third party; going through court action can be worse than suffering in silence (not least for your career). Avoid any situations where you might be alone and could be cornered.

If you are harassed, act cool and be utterly unimpressed. Restrain nervous laughter, don't even give them the time of day. Calm indifference is prime defence. Don't react – taking their bait will give them the impression they're winning the power battle.

Action Required

If the predatory behaviour persists, it's time to be more direct. You should tell them (calmly) that it is making you feel uncomfortable. Call upon the vigilance of reliable and trusted colleagues; has this bounder been chest-beating with other females? Some pests are so thick-skinned that they might not realise that their behaviour amounts to harassment. Collect the evidence and then carefully consider the form of your complaint. Go to your boss with a confident and measured account of what's happened; they should then intervene and take disciplinary measures.

If the guilty party is your boss, you should report them to another figure of authority or a company director. Don't hang back – you know when you really feel uncomfortable. If it develops into a battle, stick to your guns.

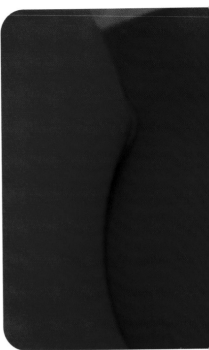

Handling the Bos

It's lonely at the top, and therein lies the boss's Achilles heel. While many fear the fence surrounding the top dog, the Girl Most Likely respects it. A first-rate relationship with your seniors requires some precision-engineering and regular maintenance. It's definitely a worthwhile investment where promotion and pay rises are the bottom line, and chummy in-jokes the bonus.

Bosses usually score the lowest on the basic How Are You enquiry rate, so it's easy to set yourself apart from more custardly colleagues. Ask after the little ones and lesser halves, but keep within polite parameters. Never ever grovel or fawn; the office creep is a social pariah.

Baseline behaviour should be calm, cheerful, polite and professional; a little measured cheekiness will counter the risk of robotics. Know your boundaries.

Careful answering back could be taken as witty repartee and disagreeing as a brave challenge, but both are unlikely to be appreciated by flaky bosses. Be the Yes-Girl and watch all the can't-dos languish in the slow lane of success. If you downplay your achievements, your humility will suggest that such genius is a daily (and indispensable) occurrence. A torrent of keenness is annoying and uncool. Discreetly let your boss know that spike in profits has your signature, but save any self-praise for one-on-one appraisals.

Bosses favour thick-skinned genes. When a work crisis erupts, ride out the panic before sharing it with the boss. They expect solutions not problems, so turn it around and, if they overrule your suggestion, all the better for you if the buck stops with them. All your fault?

Defensiveness might be instinctive but it looks rather small-minded. Resume your professionalism and calmly explain yourself; sneaking on colleagues is held as playground behaviour. All emotional entanglements should be dealt with in private – tears and trauma will make you look like the weakest link. Confide in a colleague if offloading is required.

Meekness encourages downward mobility, so override your intimidation and awkward body language. Avoid overtures that start 'sorry, can I just…?' No one respects a doormat. If prone to crumbling under nervous pressure, try to mentally rehearse conversations.

When asking for that pay rise, bide your time. Even with open-plan offices, always book a meeting. This is classic haggling territory, so invent a rival bid and go armed with a fitting sum (more than you expect). Prepare persuasive reasoning as to why a raise is deserved and firmly bookend your request with positivity and tempered outpourings of company and career satisfaction.

Resignations should be committed to a brief letter glowing with courtesy and compliments. Burning bridges will wave goodbye to good references and paths will inevitably cross again. If you anticipate a sacking, bravely consider getting in there first (or hold out for the severance jackpot). Getting the boot is superlatively humiliating, but there is yet more dignity to lose by losing your temper. Don't argue, blame or criticise. Settle for the philosophical advantage and serve out your notice with grace. Remember, at this stage, references, settlements and second chances are still valuably negotiable.

Good Boss, Bad Boss

Mutual boss hate may encourage staff bonding behind their backs, but it's far shrewder to play out a simple game of professional manipulation. Bosses are likely to be the office hate figure as most bully staff – such is the corrupting nature of power – and there are three malevolent counterparts.

First, there's the (often female) competitive boss who sees you as a threat and is a dog in the manger with opportunities. Pity their insecurities privately and then indulge them as your role model. Your flattery gives a false sense of security; ripping the rug from under their feet will then be all the easier.

Secondly, there's the cheating boss who farms out work and then steals all the credit. They are chronically insecure and professionally greedy. Ensure you set up some unwitting witnesses when offering ideas. Group emails to said boss and superiors will make all aware of your own business brilliance.

Lastly, there's the despot, who will operate in a climate of fear. Never rise to any outbursts and never stoop to combat or answer back. Wait for the storm to pass. Block out the little voice that speaks of personal offence; cool composure and detachment win the upper ground and maintain dignity. Pity is an effective rationalisation of the egomania, inability to empathise and general character deficiencies.

What if you are the boss? Whether at the very top of the pyramid, or just in charge of the tea boy, getting the most out of subordinates is evidently harder than it looks. Promotion must bring increased emotional detachment; being everyone's best friend makes any finger-wagging awkward. A charming but firm manner over cold and curt is best. Any disciplinary action must be conducted in private; any dismissals always face to face.

A dream boss should be unfeasibly calm, approachable and encouraging. She sets clear, reasonable goals and doesn't move the goalposts. She holds hands over precarious paths and gives staff a long rein when things can afford to go a bit wrong. Home-time demands only happen in emergencies. After all that wonderfulness, she should avoid any smug superiority and must employ a little self-depreciation. She must also realise that the shipment of cupcakes is a perfectly justifiable business expense; worker bees are most suggestible to loyalty with the offer of sweet food.

Socials and Away Days

Best Behaviour

Attempts to mix business with pleasure are always rather strained. The pressure is on to be a social sensation. The best plan is to max up the effort, manners and charm. Be armed with a few social icebreakers (extra-curricular activities, families, relationships – nosy but often productive). Dress up; making an effort immediately communicates a positive attitude. Try to cling on to a shred of professionalism – even in the darkest corner of the dance floor – and the ordeal will be eased (especially in retrospect).

The day after still counts. Crawling in hungover and late (or worse, pulling a sickie) is just not considered team spirit. Now is the day to bounce in on time, on the case and seemingly indestructible, though without the slightest smugness.

Socialising

It's tactical to socialise. Although it can be more fun to mix with the underlings, your boss should neither be besieged nor ignored. Maintain your professional gloss, but drop the solemnity and work the charm. You'll be observed, so crack a risqué joke, but make a judgement call. Social dormice may want to rely on a colleague, but clinging on to allies is bound by a law of diminishing returns. Some office socials come but once a year, so work it.

Pitfalls can be plentiful at in-house socials. Lurching conversation leads to unchecked alcoholic intake, and inner truths are propelled into reality (clumsy crushes, latent dislikes). The subtext of a social is a test of interpersonal skills and how you fit the company. Provided certain caveats are flagged up, all but the sociopath are better for it.

Evening Entertainments

Not usually an optional event, but just dropping in on an evening do for a spot of face time before quietly leaving may do the trick. Dress up but play it safe; adhere to form and only bring a guest if they have been invited.

Alcohol might be a key ingredient. Pre-empt situational overdoses: avoid shots, eat well, spike drinks with water. Try not to be the first man down. Steer clear of mistletoe and dirty dancing.

Thanking the host on departure will reap good marks (you can usually slip away from larger parties without too many formalities). To kiss or not to kiss goodbye? Affection can be a pleasant closure but, if you've skirted the MD all night, now is not the time to break into their personal space. If kissing of a less innocent nature is on the cards, take it off-site or you'll be tomorrow's news.

Away Days

Professionalism (or acting) is called for as you'll be on show for longer and, as time passes, you'll have to try harder to make an effort. Claustrophobia kicks in and colleagues become more irritating.

Overnight stays can complicate the coupling of alcohol and romance (any innocent hotel room encounters will be misconstrued). And since it's all about the team, there's little breathing space and usually no escape. Tasks are often humiliating, group hugs compulsory and amenities taste-free.

Ignore urges to rebel and even with jollies expect hard work, not a holiday. You'll share coach seats and headache pills with arch enemies. Remain free of any hangovers and be well-groomed at all times. It's quite a long and tedious performance, so grit those teeth and freeze that smile.

Entertaining

Joyful fact: wining and dining business contacts wins contracts. It's an excuse for expense account extravagance, but it takes rather more than flexing the company credit card to close deals.

The most uncomfortable issue can be deciphering who is host and who is guest. Officially, the inviter is the host. They should reserve the table, indicate if it's teetotal or endless wine, and also pick up the bill.

Being the wanton guest is very bad business. Always follow the host's lead in terms of cost, quantity and alcohol. Time is money, but don't rush. There's often a business matter to discuss but never raise it on the first mouthful; far shrewder to wait until you're all one course (and several drinks) down. The guest should always reward the host with gratitude (an email is usually fine).

Fundamentals

Golden Rules

ABCs

Please, thank you and sorry. Virtually the first words we're taught to say, yet still worryingly neglected. Pleases and thank yous must accompany each and every request/receipt; garnish with a casual smile for extra effect. Likewise, apologise whenever your actions have impacted negatively on other people. There is no need to overstate the case. Some simple sincerity is sufficient.

Allergies

Hosts/companions should be alerted to serious allergies/food phobias. Only those with medical conditions should bring their own supplies, and only if their requirements are inconvenient for other people.

Bodily Functions

We all have them, but they're never up for discussion.

Breakages

Own up. You must insist on paying for a replacement model (assuming it's not a family heirloom or priceless antique). The conscientious will produce a new model, or a similar object of equal or greater value, as soon as possible.

Breath

Ladies don't smell. Ever. They promptly attend to any malodorous indulgences such as cigarettes, alcohol, coffee, and garlic. They have clean, flossed teeth and a supply of mints in their handbag.

Burping

It may amuse you, but most people will find it offensive and unattractive.

Children

Offer to hold babies, but don't shriek if they vomit on your carpet. If the rug rat is being unruly, you can politely point it out, but leave parenting to the parents. When on their territory, it's rude to do anything else but put up with any brats. Don't put on baby voices with anyone past toddler age and don't patronise children. If you really find small people intolerable, arrange to see your friends after bedtime; if inviting the parents to dinner, it is acceptable not to invite the cubs (but don't forget to ask after the little darlings). N.B. only parents have the right to teach their children vulgar vocabulary.

Danger Words

A knowledge of frowned-upon words is prudent. Language is ever evolving but the following weapons of word warfare are still prevalent: loo or lavatory never toilet; napkin never serviette; supper never tea (N.B. tea is served at 4 p.m. and no later, supper is more informal than dinner and dinner is served in a dining room); sofa never settee; sitting room or drawing room, never lounge or front room (a drawing room should only exist in a house that also has a sitting room). A 'show' is an exhibition; the word should never be used to refer to a theatre production.

Diets

Never overburden a love-interest with details of your dieting regime. Never inflict your diets on others. Save it for relevant conversations/compliments.

Dress Duplication

Turned up to that coveted party to find yourself face to face with an identical outfit? Don't ignore your twin. Make the first move and initiate some humour in recognition of the situation. Rise above the humiliation and convince yourself that you look better than them.

Humour

A little bit of lightheartedness enhances everyone's day. Never take yourself too seriously; be gracious and a good sport when the joke's on you.

Illness

If you feel unwell, stay at home. Don't launch off into a detailed account about your symptoms; no one is interested in your sniffle. They'll be more concerned about how contagious you are, rather than how you're feeling.

Itches

Ladies never publicly scratch.

Lateness

Be on time, or at least arrive within the 15-minute safety window. Anything more is downright rude and, amongst friends and colleagues, will only earn you a reputation for being unreliable.

Moodiness

Huffing and puffing is unattractive and won't win you any favours. Swinging moods and declarations of boredom are reserved for teenagers. Charm is a far more powerful currency.

Mouths

Cover your mouth if yawning, coughing or sneezing. If you are accidentally spat upon, wait a minute and then slyly wipe away so as not to embarrass the culprit (unless they have drawn attention to it). If the you're the spitter, apologise at once. Expectorating publicly will result in instant relegation from lady status.

Nails

Indulge in a regular manicure. Dirty or snagged nails look unkempt. Don't bite your fingernails, or nibble at any loose skin around them. Toenails can only be exposed if they are pedicured, painted, clean and well-groomed.

Noses

Sniffing is vile to listen to. Have a good blow; never wipe your nose with your hand. All nose-picking should be done when closeted away, or by discreetly blowing into a tissue. Neither time nor tools? Use your fingers as a shield and brush away the offending article with your thumb, as swiftly as a gull catches fish. If a friend has a bogey, it's kind to alert them – 'you have something…' plus an instructive gesture should do it. Then move the conversation swiftly on.

Nudity

There's a very fine line between being painfully body shy and embarrassingly *laissez-faire*. Excessive modesty raises eyebrows as much as parading about *au naturel*. Gauge your audience and follow suit.

Pregnant Pauses

Unless you are bosom buddies, never ask a married couple if they're trying (or point out her refusal of alcohol), or assume that all pregnant women are married. Don't ask a woman when she's due unless it's unmistakable; if it's more likely to be babies than burgers, ask an obviously leading question such as: 'so, what's the news with you?'.

Public Eating

Tone down unsightly habits (chewing with your mouth open, smacking your lips, licking fingers, picking teeth) or risk putting others off their food. Never eat in the street, particularly when on the move. Walking and chewing is not a good look. It is cruel to impose food smells, sights and sounds on others in confined spaces, so avoid picnicking on the tube, commuter trains or buses.

Sex

Never boast, force facts on to those who are anything less than fascinated, or intimidate others with your implied prowess. Keep detailed discussions for girly chats. As unbelievable as it may be, no one else is interested.

Size

Never ask a man if he thinks you're fat. Being self-assured and shapely is far more appealing than being scrawny and screwy. N.B. unless above average, also don't talk about his 'size'.

Spillages

Apologise. Clean up immediately and offer to pay for any damage. If it's on someone else's cream linen trousers, insist on picking up the dry cleaning bill. If prone to accidental slopping and spilling, avoid red wine.

Swearing

Salty language is losing its shock value, but there are times when only a good swear word will do (as a description, of course, and not an insult). Swearing is most improper at ceremonies, in job interviews and in front of younger or older generations. A good rescue is to convert profanities (mid-blurt) into a pre-prepared bank of similar-sounding words: for example, 'shucks', 'what a muck-up' or 'oh fudge'.

Wind

Blame the dog. Even if there isn't one.

Zzzzz

Make sure you get sufficient shut-eye; tiredness dims your inner glow and dulls your sparkle. Tempers are likely to be frayed and your usual cool lost. N.B. dropping off in public should be reserved for aeroplanes.

Picture Credits

Acknowledgements

Debrett's would like to thank:

Arezoo Kaviani
Boodles
Caviar House & Prunier
Charles Worthington Salons
Colour me Beautiful
NetJets
Rigby & Peller
Smythson
The Blue Bar at The Berkeley
The Elizabeth Arden Red Door
   Salon & Spa
The Suzy Lamplugh Trust
Topshop Style Advisor Service
Umu
YO! Sushi

The Publisher would particularly like to thank:

Polly Arnold
Susan Shulman
Roger Hawkins
Amy Tipper

and for their help with images:

Rick Mayston
Stephanie Molloy
Mirja Renner

With special thanks to Tom Bryant

'I can't believe she hasn't mentioned *moi*.' The acknowledgements page of an etiquette guide is quite the test on its author. Here, insurance apologies for inevitable omissions must precede any thanks. Thus, to all the *mois*, my abject apologies. Others, of course, may prefer not to be mentioned by name – to all those brilliantly rebellious friends whose disregard of decorum might, just might, have inspired the 'don'ts' of this guide, thank you.

There are many pure thanks to dispense – firstly to my sister Sophie Biggs and friend Spoon Newell, who served as my primary editors and fished out all the malapropisms and turned around the terrible sense from my first draft; to my other sister Chloe Stirling and her husband James who endured session after session of brainstorming; to my parents who set me straight on matters too sophisticated for me to grasp; to Aurora Shulman who leaked my telephone number to Ian Castello-Cortes in the first place; to Oli Barrett for his expert networking knowledge, and to my dear friends who patiently sat through long car journeys, picky phone calls and sabotaged nights out to settle my etiquette quandaries (in no particular order): Abid David, Marianne Bak-Jensen, Cara MacDowall, Jessie Brinton, Annabee Hood, Talib Choudhry, Ollie Wright, Jason Morris, Tristram Biggs, Rob Shaw, Leanne Silver, Mark and Sammy Cole, Matt and Lucia Williams, Helen Brown, Sina Sarikhani, Milly Snell, Grae Hillary, Gemma Soames, Adam Thompson and Camilla Stoddart.

And, of course, I am extremely grateful to Debrett's for the honour of writing this book – to Ian Castello-Cortes for his brilliant navigation, and to Jo Aitchison and Eleanor Mathieson for their guidance and the fruits of their research.

This guide also owes thanks to the authors of numerous books around the subject from which much good sense was gleaned: *Etiquette in Society, in Business, in Politics and at Home* by Emily Post, *Debrett's New Guide to Etiquette and Modern Manners* by John Morgan, *Talk to the Hand* by Lynne Truss, *Blaikie's Guide to Modern Manners* by Thomas Blaikie, *Things and More Things you Need to be Told* by the Etiquette Grrls, *How to Walk in High Heels* by Camilla Morton, *The Fabulous Girl's Guide to Decorum* by Kim Izzo and Ceri Marsh, *Manners* by Kate Spade, *The Wine Book* by Matthew Jukes, *Watching the English* by Kate Fox, and the *Lying Ape* by Brian King.

FLEUR BRITTEN

Index

Index

A

Accessories 41, 44–45
  beachwear 98–99
  belt 41
  black tie event 44
  everyday 41
  formal event 44
  gloves 41, 45
  handbag 41, 44, 45
  hat 41, 46
  investing in 41
  jewellery 41, 45
  scarf 41
  smart casual 46
  society event 46
  sunglasses 41
  watch 41
  white tie event 45
  wrap 45
Accidents
  breakages 210
  spillages 211
Aeroplanes 74, 102, 211
Affairs 140, 200–01
Age, revealing one's 176
Alcohol 93
  aperitifs 52, 71
  at drinks parties 157
  at work events 206–07
  bars 88
  buying rounds 88, 131
  port etiquette 87
  spirits 71
  toasts 86, 88
  wine and champagne 64–69
  wine glasses 52
Allergies 210

Apologising 210
Appearance 24–47
Arguments 16, 176
  at work 197
  over money 136
  with friends 20
Arrogance 180
Ascot 46

B

Ballet 46
Bars 88
  hotel 105
Beach 98–99
  holiday 136
Beauty treatments
  bikini wax 79
  eyebrow wax 33
  manicure 33, 79, 149, 211
  massage 78–79
  pedicure 33, 79, 98, 211
  spa 78–79
Bitching 182
Blind dates 124
Bluffing, social 181
Bodily functions
  burping 210
  coughing 211
  scratching 210
  sniffing 211
  sneezing 211
  wind 211
  yawning 211
Body language 14
  flirting 117–18
  in bars 88

  in restaurants 82–83
  in social situations 174
  in the office 203
  laughter 10, 13
  men's 118
  smiling 10, 14
Boyfriends 114–51
  arguing with 136, 138
  business trip with 128–29
  cohabitation 139
  communication 127, 146
  conduct in public 138–39
  dating 120–21
  flirting 117–18
  healthy relationship 138–39, 146–47
  his ex 138–39
  holidays 132–33, 136
  introducing him to your parents 135
  meeting his friends 130–31
  meeting his parents 134–35
  nagging 147
  office affairs 200–01
  public displays of affection 138
  seduction 117–18, 123
  sleeping with 126–27
  splitting up 143, 150, 201
  understanding men 146–47
  your ex 144
Business trip 207
  accompanying your man 128–29
  hotels 105

C

Camping 96
Career 194–207
  See also Work

Celebrities, meeting 91, 113
Champagne 68–69
Chopsticks 58–59
Children
    other people's 210
Cleavage, enhancing 30
Clothes
    See also Dress
    beachwear 98–99
    borrowing friends' 29, 164
    cashmere 26
    flattering styles 30
    heels 26, 38–39
    jeans 30, 37, 46
    linen 46
    shoes 26, 38–39
    silk 26, 30, 41
    tweed 30
    underwear 26, 36–37
Clubbing 90–91
Cohabitation 139
    See also Flatmates
Complaining
    in hotels 105
    in restaurants 51, 83
Conversation, art of 170–81
    arguments 177
    awkward silences 177
    bluffing 181
    business jargon 180
    escaping from bores 179, 180
    flattery 179
    foreign words 180
    introducing people 170
    joke-telling 179
    meeting people 170–73
    nosiness 176

    political correctness 176
    saying the wrong thing 176, 211
Countryside pursuits 166–67

D

Dancing
    shoes 39
    clubbing 90–91
Dating 120–27
    being stood up 17, 145
    blind 124
    cancelling 17
    first dates 120–21
    internet 124
    kissing 120, 121
    speed 124
    standing someone up 17, 145
    staying the night 126–27
    what to wear 120, 124
    who pays? 121, 133
Deportment 12–16
    formal dinners 86–87
    in aeroplanes 74
    in bars 88
    in cars 75
    in private jets 102
    in shoes 38
    on a yacht 100–01
    on public transport 75
    on the beach 99
Diamonds
    affordable alternatives 41
    engagement ring 149
Diets, discussing 210
Dinner parties
    attending 162–63

cancelling 17
crockery and cutlery 52–53
hosting 154–55, 159
napkins 53
punctuality 16–17
smoking at 92
table manners 51
Doors, holding open 13, 14
Dress 16, 24–47
See also Dress codes; Clothes
accessories 41, 44–45
beachwear 98–99
black tie event 44
boating 100–01
classics 30
cocktail 45
countryside 167
date 120, 124
elegance 29
experimenting 26, 41
fashion principles 26–27
gym 76
holiday 105, 136
making first impressions 29, 82, 90, 120, 124
off-the-peg 30
originality 30
power dressing 26, 29
rules 30
spa 78
underwear 36–37
white tie event 45
work away days 206
work 197
Dress codes 44–45
black tie event 44
dinner party 154

'formal daywear' 46
hotel 105
nightclub 90
polo 109
'smart casual' 46
'smart day' 46
society event 46
theatre, opera, ballet 46
wedding 46
white tie event 45
Driving 75
Drugs 155
Drunkenness 93
Dutch, going 121, 133

E
Eating, in public 211
Eavesdropping 182
Email 192–93
at work 197
invitations 154, 186
Engagement 148–50
announcing 150
ending 150
length 150
parents' permission 148
party 150
ring 149
sending congratulations 150
Entertaining 154–63
business event 207
dinner party 159
drinks party 156–57
house guests 160–63
picnic 106–07
restaurant get-together 82–85

smoking 92
unexpected guests 155, 161
Environment, respecting 97, 99, 167
Ex 139, 143
bumping into 144
meeting your man's 138–39
Eye contact 14, 173
Eyebrows 33

F
Fake tan 33, 136
Fashion *See* Dress; Style
Feminism 14
Festivals 96–97
Flatmates 141, 164
Flirting 117–18, 146
Flying 74, 102
Food and drink 48–71
canapés 55
crockery and cutlery 52–53
dinner party 159
drinks party 157
eating awkward food 55–63
formal dinner 86–87
napkin 53
picnic 106–07
port etiquette 87
restaurant 82–83
seafood 60–63
spirits 71
sushi 58–59
table manners 51, 82–83
wine and champagne 52, 64–69
Foreign languages 180
Formal dinner 86–87
Friends 18–20

and money 80
borrowing clothes 29, 164
dating a friend's ex 139
holidaying with 105
introducing your man to 131
living with 141, 164
meeting your man's 130–31
versus boyfriend 138–39
with your ex 144

G

Gender politics 14
Gifts
    giving 22–23
    receiving 23
    recycling 23
Gossip 182
    office 197
Grooming, personal 16, 78
    exposed body parts 30
    for the beach 98
    for overnight stays 126
Guests
    dinner party 159
    drinks party 156–57
    house 154–55, 160–67
    if you are the guest 162–63, 166–67
    unexpected 155, 161
Gym 76–77

H

Hair 34–35, 45
    and hats 41
    and open-top cars 35

flattering styles 35
hairdresser 34–35
holiday 136
Hangovers 51, 207
Harassment, at work 201
Hats 29, 41
    Ascot 46
    weddings 46
Henley 46
Holidays
    camping 96
    country break 166–67
    mini-break 132–33
    romantic getaway 136
    self-catering 105
    with friends 105
Hotels 105
House guests
    hosting 160–61
    if you are the guest 134–35, 162–63, 166–67
Humour, day to day 210
Hygiene, personal 16, 210
    and perfume 41
    and shoes 39
    at festivals 96–97

I

Illness, discussing 210
Infidelity 140, 200–01
Internet dating 124
Introductions 170
Invitations 154, 186
    responding to 186
    wedding 150
    writing 186

I

Jewellery 41, 45

K

Kissing
- at work 198, 206
- on a date 120, 121
- potential date material 117
- public displays of affection 138
- social 173, 198
- wearing a hat 41, 173

L

Language, bad 211
- no-no words 210
Letter-writing 190–91
- Christmas cards 191
- condolence letters 191
- email 192–93
- postcards 191
- presentation 190
- responding to invitations 186
- sending invitations 186
- stationery 189
- thank you letters 190
Lift/elevator, behaviour in 13
Love
- dating 120–24
- healthy relationships 138–39, 146–47
- office romance 200–01
- saying 'I love you' 147
Lying 182

M

Make-up 30–33
- beach 99
- daytime 32
- evening 32
- holiday 136
- subtle 26, 32
Manicure 33, 79, 149
Manners 10–17
- table 51, 56–57, 82–83, 86–87, 106–07
Marriage
- affairs 140
- engagement 150
- parents' permission 148
- proposals 148–49
Massage 78–79
Matchmaking 124
Media and fashion 27
Men 114–51
- art of seduction 117–18, 123
- being dumped 143
- blind dates 124
- business trips with 128–29
- chat-up lines 117
- cohabitation 139
- commitment-phobes 147, 150
- dating 120–24
- dumping 143
- flirting 117–18
- how to understand 146
- meeting his friends 130–31
- meeting his parents 134–35
- mini-break 132–33
- office affair 200–01
- one-night stand 122–23
- perfume and 42
- sleeping with 126–27
Mini-break 132–33, 105
Mobile phone
- and lateness 17
- using at work 198
- using on public transport 75
Money 80
- and romance 133, 136
- arguing about 136
- buying rounds of drinks 88, 131
- cohabitation 139
- going Dutch 121, 133
- pay rises 203
- paying in restaurants 85, 121
- salary, discussing 80, 197
Mood swings 211

N

Nails 33, 149, 211
Name
- dropping 180
- forgetting someone's 170
Nightclubs 90–91
Nudity
- at a spa 78–79
- at the gym 76–77
- in front of others 211
Modesty 180
Music
- clubbing 90–91
- festivals 96–97
- opera 111
- parties 157
- pop concerts 111

O

Office politics 197
Office romance 200–01
One-night stands 122–23
Opera-going 111
    dress code 46

P

Pampering 78–79
Parties
    art of conversation 170–83
    attending 162–63
    canapés 55
    dinner 159
    drinks 156–57
    engagement 150
    escaping from bores 179, 180
    hosting, general 154–55
    in a shared flat 164
    invitations 154, 186
    meeting new people 170–71
    work-related 206
Pedicure 33, 79, 98, 211
Perfume 42
Personal trainer 77
Picnic 106–07, 111
    formal 107
    hosting 106
    what to take 106–07
Politeness 10
Political correctness 176
Polo 108–09
Pop concerts 111
Posture 12–14
    See also Deportment

Power dressing 26
Pregnancy
    mistaken 211
    on public transport 75
Presents
    See Gifts
Private jets 102
Professionalism 197, 203, 206–07
Proposal, marriage 148–49
Public persona 16
Punctuality 16–17, 210
    on dates 120

Q

Queueing 13

R

Relationships 114–51
    arguing 136, 138
    art of seduction 117–18
    at work 200–01
    cohabitation 139
    communication 127, 146
    dating 120–21
    engagement 150
    exes 138–39, 143–144
    flirting 117–18
    healthy 138–39, 146–47
    infidelity 140
    introducing him to your parents 135
    marriage proposals 148–49
    meeting his friends 130–31
    meeting his parents 134–35
    office affairs 200–01
    splitting up 143, 150, 201

understanding men 146–47
Relaxation
See also Holiday
spas 78–79
Restaurants 82–85, 105
See also Food; Wine
booking 82
crockery and cutlery 52–53
paying 85
punctuality 16–17
smoking 92
sushi 58–59
table manners 51, 53, 82–83
Retail therapy 26
Romance
dating 120–24
flirting 117–18
holidays 132–33, 136
office 200–01
Royalty 112
addressing 112
RSVPs 186

S

Seduction, art of 117–18, 123
Self-confidence 13, 32, 44
Sex
discussing with others 211
in flagrante 141
one-night stands 122–23
with a new man 126–27
with an ex 143
with friends 147
Shaking hands 173
with royalty 112
Shoes 38–39, 45
and pedicures 38
care of 39
deportment 38

storage 39
Sleep, importance of 211
Smoking 87, 92
Social graces 8–23, 170–83, 210–211
Space, personal 13
Spas 78–79
Spitting 211
Sport
gym 76–77
polo 108–09
yachting 100–01
yoga 77
Stationery 189
Style 26–30
See also Dress
Swimwear
on a beach 98–99
on a yacht 100–01

T

Table manners 51, 56–57
canapés 55
formal dinners 86–87
napkins 53
picnics 106–07
restaurants 82–83
Tablewear
crockery and cutlery 52–53
napkins 53
wine glasses 52
Telephone 197
invitations 154, 186
personal calls at work 197
procuring a man's number 117
Thank you letters 190
Theatre-going 111
dress code 46
Time-keeping 210
Tipping 80

bar staff 88
bellboy 105
cloakroom attendant 90
doorman 105
hairdresser 35
in a hotel 105
on a yacht 101
porter 105
waiter 85
Toasts 69, 86, 88
Tradition and chivalry 10, 14, 159
Transport
aeroplanes 74, 102, 211
cars 75
public 75
taxis 75
walking 75
yachting 100–01
Travel
See Holiday; Transport

U

Underwear 26, 36–37, 126

W

Waxing
bikini 79
eyebrows 33
Wedding
calling off 150
dress code 41, 46
list 22
presents 22
Weekend break
business trip 128–29
countryside 166–67
romantic 132–33
Weight, discussing 211

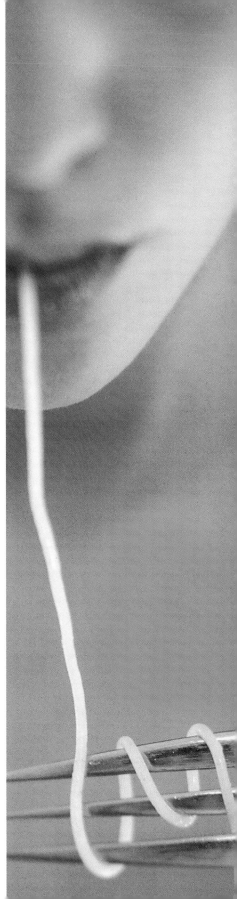

Wine 64–69
    champagne 68–69
    choosing 65–66
    glasses 52, 65, 68–69
    list 65
    mixing 65
    opening 65, 68
    ordering 65–66
    serving 66, 68
    tasting 66
Work 194–207
    away days 207
    being the boss 204
    body language 203
    business jargon 180
    business lunches 207
    career advancement 197–203
    cigarette break 92
    confidentiality 197
    confrontation 197
    crises 203
    dress 197, 206
    duvet days 198
    email 192–93, 197
    entertaining 207
    flirting with colleagues 200
    harassment 197, 201
    hierarchy 197
    lunch breaks 197
    meetings 198
    office gossip 197
    office politics 197
    office romance 200–01
    pay rise 203
    personal phone calls 197
    personal space 13
    popularity at 198
    professionalism 197, 203, 206–07
    punctuality 198
    resignation 203

    sacking 203
    sick days 182, 198, 206
    socialising with colleagues 206
    socials 206
    survival skills 197–98
    telephone 197
    your boss 200, 202–04
Writing, art of 184–93
    Christmas cards 191
    condolence letters 191
    email 192–93
    postcards 191
    presentation 190
    responding to invitations 186
    sending invitations 186
    stationery 189
    thank you letters 190

Y

Yachting 100–01
Yoga 77